Who Are You to Judge?

Who Are You to Judge?

The Dangers of Judging and Legalism

Dave Swavely

PUBLISHING
P.O. BOX 817 • PHILLIPSBURG • NEW JERSEY 08865-0817

Unless otherwise indicated, Scripture quotations are from the NEW AMERICAN STANDARD BIBLE®. Copyright © 1960, 1962, 1963, 1968, 1971, 1972, 1973, 1975, 1977, 1995 by The Lockman Foundation. Used by permission.

Page design and typesetting by Lakeside Design Plus

Printed in the United States of America

Library of Congress Cataloging-in-Publication Data

Swavely, David, 1966–
    Who are you to judge? : the dangers of judging and legalism / Dave Swavely.
        p. cm.
    Includes bibliographical references and index.
    ISBN-13: 978-1-59638–011-0 (pbk.)
    ISBN-10: 1-59638-011-X (pbk.)
    1. Bible. N.T. Corinthians, 1st. IV, 3–7—Criticism, interpretation, etc. 2. Judgment—Religious aspects—Christianity.
3. Grace (Theology) 4. Toleration—Religious aspects.
5. Discrimination—Religious aspects—Christianity. 6. Religious tolerance. 7. Christian life. I. Title.

BS2675.52.S93 2005
241—dc22

                                                                2005052131

To C. W. Smith,
my college professor who first introduced me
to Paul's words in 1 Corinthians 4:5–6 and
insisted on their application with a humble tenacity

Contents

Introduction

T he words "judging" and "legalism" are often used but seldom understood. They can have a different meaning almost every time they are spoken.

Over the years in my ministry as a pastor, people have told me, "What I like about you, Dave, is that you are not judgmental." But other people have told me that I am too judgmental. Some have said that they like our church because it is not legalistic, but others have said they would never attend our church because it is too legalistic. So am I judgmental, or not? Are we legalistic, or what?

Obviously there is a problem of definition when it comes to these terms. So one of the goals of this book is to attempt to define them in a biblical manner. What does God mean when He talks about "judging," or addresses the problem of "legalism"? If we can understand what the Bible says about these issues, then hopefully we can all discuss and address them from God's perspective, and avoid the confusion illustrated above.

Another goal of this book is to recover two important biblical commands, and the principles related to them, that have been largely neglected in the church of Jesus Christ. These commands are summarized in the words of the apostle Paul in 1 Corinthians 4:5–6, where he says that we should not judge one another, and that we should not "go beyond what is written" (NIV, ESV). The Lord Jesus also repeatedly addressed these issues during His earthly ministry, as we will learn later in the book. But although many Christians are very concerned about keeping the other commands in Scripture, like those found in the Ten Commandments, very few seem to be worried about these. In fact, I would say that there are as much disregard and disobedience of these commands of Scripture as of any other, and it is often the most spiritual people who are at fault. In fact, it seems to me that the most committed Christians are actually more susceptible to this problem than are those who are not as strong.

The sin of judging is a root cause in most of the inter-personal conflicts that arise in the lives of believers, and so learning to identify and avoid this sin will go a long way toward promoting peace and joy in the body of Christ. And legalism, which is the institutional form of judging, is a dangerous disease that plagues many of our Christian institutions, from churches to schools to families, sapping their spiritual strength and weakening the work of God in their midst.

Here are some examples of judgmental and legalistic statements that I have heard from Christians, all of which we will discuss at some point in this book:

"I know what you're thinking," or "I know why you did that."

"There is no way someone can drive a car that expensive and be a godly man."

"Rock music is the devil's music and is never appropriate for a Christian."

"A church that does not serve weekly communion is dishonoring the Lord."

"Any woman who works a full-time job is neglecting her children."

"R-rated movies are not an option for a believer."

"Modern alcoholic drinks are more potent than the wine of Jesus' day, so we should not drink them."

"It is a sin to send your children to a public school."

"God is sickened by the singing of simplistic praise choruses that repeat the same words over and over."

"People who take Prozac and other psychiatric medications are not trusting God."

"It's wrong to watch football on the Sabbath Day."

"Birth control robs God of His sovereignty and rebelliously refuses His blessings."

"Smoking is a sin, because it destroys the temple of God."

"The person who practices the discipline of fasting is more spiritual than the person who does not."

"If you feed your baby 'on demand' or let your child sleep in the bed with you, you are bad parents."

"She's a member of our church, but I don't think she's a true Christian."

I have thought and said some of those statements myself at different times in my life, but I now believe that all of them are wrong in some way. The issues they address are important for Christians to carefully consider, but the problem is that all of those statements "go beyond what is written" by making spiritual judgments and creating moral standards outside of what God has revealed to us. A person who falls into that error is often failing to recognize the distinction between being "fully convinced in his own mind" (Rom. 14:5) and being careful not to judge his brother (Rom. 14:13). And that problem creates many other problems in our lives, as we will learn.

You also may have thought or said some of the statements above, and may not see anything wrong with them.

If that is the case, I encourage you to keep an open mind as you read this book, asking God to give you His perspective on these things. And even if none of those examples apply to you, I am sure there are other ways that you will be tempted to judge others, or to "go beyond what is written." This has been a problem for all Christians since the days of Christ, and it will be a problem until the day He returns.

On the other hand, you probably have been judged by other Christians at some point in your life, and found that to be a confusing experience. This book will help you to understand what judgments are right and necessary, and which ones are inappropriate according to the Word of God. You may also have labored under a load of legalistic laws, wondering which ones are really necessary to keep. This book will help you with that problem as well. Perhaps in reading it you will have the joyous and liberating experience of finding out that the negative opinions and rules of God's people are not necessarily the opinions and rules of God Himself!

The Case against Judging

I n 1 Corinthians 4:3–7 the apostle Paul says:

> To me it is a very small thing that I should be examined by
> you, or by any human court; in fact, I do not even exam-
> ine myself. For I am conscious of nothing against myself,
> yet I am not by this acquitted; but the one who examines
> me is the Lord. Therefore do not go on passing judgment
> before the time, but wait until the Lord comes who will
> both bring to light the things hidden in the darkness and
> disclose the motives of men's hearts; and then each man's
> praise will come to him from God.
>
> Now these things, brethren, I have figuratively applied
> to myself and Apollos for your sakes, so that in us you may
> learn not to exceed what is written, so that no one of you
> will become arrogant in behalf of one against the other.
> For who regards you as superior? What do you have that
> you did not receive? And if you did receive it, why do you
> boast as if you had not received it?

This passage, as much as any other in Scripture, has
helped me to understand how to think about difficult
issues in the Christian life, and how to promote unity and
peace among my brothers and sisters in the Lord. But I
have been surprised to find that it is relatively unknown

to many Christians, who have not studied or been taught the rich truth contained in it. So in an effort to rediscover these profound words of the apostle Paul, I will be using this passage as the framework for the first six chapters of this book. At the very least, when you are finished reading it, I hope you will know what this text of Scripture says, what it means, and how it applies to your life.

Judging on Trial

Paul begins this section of his letter to the church at Corinth by addressing a problem that he calls "judging," which is a root problem in the sense that so many other problems proceed from it. Wouldn't it be better to fight a fire when it has first started, rather than after it has become a raging inferno? And wouldn't you rather pluck out the weeds while they are young, before they have completely overgrown your garden? In the same way, much of the worst conflict, bitterness, and prejudice among people begins its development with the practice of wrongful judging. But if we can learn to identify and avoid this root problem, it will never blossom into such foul fruit.

Before we consider Paul's case against judging, it would be good to define the words he uses to refer to this problem. What exactly is the "judging" that is commanded against? Three times in verses 3–4 we find forms of the Greek verb *anakrinō*, which is translated "examine" by the NASB. This is a term that speaks of evaluating someone or something and then reaching a positive or negative conclusion. For instance, it is used in 1 Corinthians 2:15, where Paul says that "he who is spiritual *appraises* all things." When the spiritual man appraises or evaluates any particular thing, the conclusion he reaches can be either commendatory or critical. We also know that the "examining" referred to by Paul in 4:3–4 can be either right or wrong, depending on the situation. After all, the end of verse 4 says that God does it, so it cannot necessarily be a sin!

In verse 5, however, Paul is clearly speaking of a *negative* judgment about someone else, which is made in the mind and often expressed through critical words. The judging referred to here is clearly something that is wrong to do, because Paul says we should stop doing it. In this verse he uses a related but slightly different Greek word—*krinō*. It is difficult to determine exactly why he chose to drop the prefix in this usage, but perhaps the former term focuses more on the evaluation process, and this one more on the conclusion that is reached. Perhaps he wanted to make it clear that he was not condemning the mere act of "examining" or evaluating someone. It is judging in the sense of reaching a conclusion, or "passing sentence" in our minds, that he is warning against.[1]

But in what situations is it wrong to pass judgment in our minds about another person? This question must be asked, because we find Paul using the same word in a neutral sense elsewhere, even in the same book of 1 Corinthians (5:3; 5:12; 6:2–3; 10:15; 11:13, etc.). Making a judgment about someone—even a negative one—is not wrong in itself, so how do we know when it is right and when it is not? The answer lies in what we are judging, or to put it another way, in the basis for our judgments. Later in the same verse (1 Cor. 4:5), Paul tells us what we cannot and should not judge about another person: "the things hidden in the darkness and . . . the motives of men's hearts." We will discuss this part of the passage in more depth later, but for now it provides the basis for a definition of the sin of judging, so we can understand what we are talking about from the beginning.

The sin of judging is *negatively evaluating someone's conduct or spiritual state on the basis of nonbiblical standards or suspected motives.* Or if that is too formal for you, here is a more colloquial version: To "judge" others is to decide that they are doing wrong because they do something the Bible doesn't talk about or because you think you can guess what is in their heart. That is what Paul means by "judging," and that is what I mean when I use the term throughout this book.

The Opening Argument

In verses 3–4 Paul begins his case against judging by explaining and illustrating the *limitations* of human judgment. He writes, "To me it is a very small thing that I may be examined by you, or by any human court." In our way of speaking, he is saying "It's no big deal if you judge me; I'm not going to lose any sleep over it." Why would Paul be so unconcerned about the opinions of the Corinthians, or any other "human court"? Because human beings are severely limited when we try to evaluate one another. We do not know everything we need to know to reach an accurate conclusion, and on top of that we are prone to misunderstand the facts that we do observe.

When I was writing this book, a series of commercials for Ameriquest Mortgage Company made their debut on TV. The tag line was "Don't judge too quickly," and the scenes in the commercials illustrated how easy it is for us to misunderstand the facts in a situation, even though they may seem patently obvious to an observer. The best (and funniest) of the commercials shows a man entering a convenience store while talking to his friend on his cell phone; he is wearing one of those hands-free ear sets that are not very visible to others. As he approaches the counter, he is commenting on a purchase that his friend has been telling him about, and he says, "You're getting robbed." Then as he reaches into his jacket for his wallet to buy something at the counter, he repeats more loudly, "Did you hear me? You're getting robbed!" Suddenly the man behind the counter maces him in the eyes, then hits him with a baseball bat while another worker rushes out from the back with a cattle prod of all things, and lets him have it with the prod as he writhes on the floor yelling, "Stop! Stop!" Then the words flash on the screen, "Don't judge too quickly."

In another one of the commercials a man lets himself into his girlfriend's apartment so he can surprise her with a nice spaghetti meal when she comes home. He sets the table with flowers and nurses the dinner in the kitchen. But just as his girlfriend arrives and is entering the apartment, her fluffy white cat knocks the saucepan off the stove, and then jumps into the splattered puddle on the floor. The man scrambles to pick up the cat by the scruff of its neck with one hand, while in the other he holds a big knife he had been using to cut the meat. So when his girlfriend turns the corner into the kitchen, she sees him holding the red-soaked cat over a pool of red liquid, which along with the knife in his other hand makes him look like a psychotic cat murderer! And again the screen says, "Don't judge too quickly."

I once had an experience like that, which illustrates the limitations of human judgment. Shortly after I had moved from Pennsylvania to California to attend seminary, I met a nice older couple after a church service. They were so friendly, I felt right at home with them. So when we were saying goodbye at the end of the conversation, I said half-jokingly, "You can have me over for dinner sometime, since I'm a starving student." They thought this was funny, so they did call me and invite me to join their family for Thanksgiving dinner. When the day came, and I was driving to their house, I was thinking about what it would be like, because this was my first social occasion with Christians from California. And my mind happened to run across the issue of alcohol. I wondered if they would be serving it, because one thing I had heard people in Pennsylvania say about people in California was, "They all drink out there." "Even the Christians drink out there," someone had said.

I had been raised in a church culture and attended a college where no one drank alcohol—it was considered a sin to do so. I did not agree theoretically that it was a sin to drink, but I also had never done it myself or been with Christians who did. And I did not personally like the taste of alcohol—it reminded me too much of the Nyquil I had to take when I had a cold! So I wondered, what should I do if they served alcohol at dinner? And I decided that I would politely refuse, but be careful not to make a scene about it.

After I arrived at the large gathering and was introduced to various members of the family, I stood on the porch for a while talking to a few of them. I glanced back inside the dining room and saw Jim, the host, circling the big table, pouring a bubbly liquid into wine glasses in front of each place setting. "So it's true," I thought, reminding myself not to be judgmental. And Jim was a deacon in my new church, by the way, so I thought, "Even the church officers drink in California!" I didn't think there was anything wrong with it, but I still felt uncomfortable, because it was a new situation for me. I tried to act nonchalant, even when they seated me right next to the host, in full view of the big crowd of strangers around the table. They had to look through me to see Jim when he reached for his wine glass and proposed a toast.

All the others grabbed their wine glasses and hoisted them in the air, except for me. In my nervousness I didn't know what to do, so I belatedly picked up my glass of water, which was shaped noticeably different from the wine glasses, of course. I held the water up with a shaking hand. *Everyone* noticed. With a funny look on his face, Jim pressed on with his toast, and then it was down the hatch for everyone. I sipped my water and set it back down in front of me.

After a few moments of almost unbearable silence, Jim said to me, "You know, Dave, that's sparkling cider."

Besides touching on an issue that has been an occasion for much judging on the part of Christians (which we will discuss later), that story is a good illustration of Paul's point in 1 Corinthians 4:3. If only I had known what was in those wine glasses, it would have saved me a lot of embarrassment. If only I could have seen inside my new friend's mind and heart, I wouldn't have looked like such a fool on that Thanksgiving Day. But remember, in *every* interaction you have with other people, you are subject to the same limitations. You seldom have all the facts, and you are certainly not privy to the thoughts rattling around inside someone's head. This is why Paul says that the judgments of other human beings are "no big deal." Our judgments about others are always limited in some way.

How Well Do You Know Yourself?

In 1 Corinthians 4:4 Paul goes even further to say that our judgments are limited in regard to *ourselves*. "In fact," he says, "I do not even examine myself. For I am conscious of nothing against myself, yet I am not by this acquitted;

but the one who examines me is the Lord." Only God knows for sure whether we are doing the right thing or not, according to Paul. We could have a clear conscience, unaware of committing any sin against God, but we could still be sinning! We simply cannot know ourselves completely at all times, or even come close to it. As Charles Spurgeon writes:

> Self examination is not the simple thing which, at first sight, it might appear. No Christian who has ever really practised it has found it easy. Is there any exercise of the soul which any one of us has found so unsatisfactory, so almost impossible, as self examination? The fact is this, that the heart is so exceedingly complicated and intricate, and it is so very near the eye which has to investigate it, and both it and the eye are so restless and so shifting, that its deep anatomy baffles our research. Just a few things, here and there, broad and open, and floating upon the surface, a man discovers; but there are chambers receding within chambers, in that deepest of all deep things, a sinner's heart, which no mere human investigation ever will reach . . . it is the prerogative of God alone to "search" the human heart.[2]

Paul's words in 1 Corinthians echo those of Jeremiah the prophet, who wrote: "The heart is more deceitful than all else and is desperately sick; who can understand it? I, the LORD, search the heart, I test the mind, even to give to each man according to his ways, according to the results of his deeds" (Jer. 17:9–10).

God Himself is the only one capable of accurately and consistently judging what is in our hearts, because He understands us better than we understand ourselves. We can be deceived about our own motives, because sin still dwells within us (Rom. 7:14–24; 1 John 1:8), and that sin can pervert our perspective on ourselves. In addition, we do not yet know everything the Bible says about what is right and what is wrong—we are all in a process of learning the meaning and application of God's commands. So, as Paul might say, we have sins in places where we don't even know we have places!

The point he is making to the Corinthians should be obvious: If we cannot even judge ourselves accurately, then we ought to be extremely careful about how we judge others. Since you cannot know with certainty what is in your *own heart*, how could you possibly think that you can discern what is in the heart of another?! And the fact that we usually do not know all the facts should produce in us a "holy hesitation" before we draw any conclusions about others. Proverbs 18 is filled with wisdom about this issue:

> A fool does not delight in understanding, but only in revealing his own mind. (v. 2)

> He who gives an answer before he hears, it is folly and shame to him. (v. 13)

> The first to plead his case seems right, until another comes and examines him. (v. 17)

This does not mean that we can never make a negative judgment about another person, of course. As I mentioned before, the Scripture calls on us to do just that at times. But because of our human limitations, we must be careful that we "not judge according to appearance, but judge with righteous judgment," as our Lord Jesus said in John 7:24. And in the words of his brother James, we should be "quick to hear, slow to speak" (James 1:19).

Judging Is a Sin

Having set the stage for his case, Paul directly addresses the practice of judging in verse 5: "Therefore do not go on passing judgment." The verb tense he uses indicates that the Corinthians had been doing this already and needed to stop doing it (see chapter 4 for an explanation of the situation at Corinth). And by commanding them to stop it, with words inspired by the Holy Spirit Himself, Paul is making it clear that judging is a sin against God—not to mention a sin against others. This is an important point to emphasize, because there seems to be widespread ignorance among God's people about this sin. Everyone knows that murder, adultery, hate, lust, and other common sins are wrong, but few are aware that it is equally wrong to judge another Christian.

In many years of pastoral counseling, I have repeatedly found that the difficulties people face in their marriages, families, churches, and jobs can be traced back to wrongful judgments that have been made in their minds concerning others. And almost as often I have found that these people are not even aware that this problem exists, or that it is a primary cause of their conflicts. But when they have learned about it, I am glad to say that through repentance from this sin and practicing new ways of thinking, many of them have experienced peace as never before, in their hearts and in their relationships with others.

This sin is so damaging to us, and displeasing to God, that the Scriptures are filled with commands against it. In addition to the prohibition in our passage, consider these others:

Do not judge so that you will not be judged. For in the way you judge, you will be judged; and by your standard of measure, it will be measured to you. (Matt. 7:1–2)

But you, why do you judge your brother? Or you again, why do you regard your brother with contempt? For we will all stand before the judgment seat of God. . . . Therefore let us not judge one another anymore. (Rom. 14:10, 13)

Do not speak against one another, brethren. He who speaks against a brother or judges his brother, speaks against the law and judges the law. . . . There is only one Lawgiver and Judge, the One who is able to save and to destroy; but who are you who judge your neighbor? (James 4:11–12)

The words in Matthew 7:1–2 are the words of our Lord Jesus, of course, and a case could be made that one of the major goals of His earthly ministry was to confront the errors of judging (the personal sin between individuals) and legalism (the institutionalized form of judging). In chapter 7 we will discuss Jesus' ministry further, but as we continue now through 1 Corinthians 4, we will learn more about the nature of sinful judging, and how to avoid it.

Matthew Henry, the great Puritan commentator, provides a summary of what we have learned so far, and a good transition to the next chapter. Writing about the command at the beginning of 1 Corinthians 4:5, he says:

The apostle takes occasion hence to caution the Corinthians against censoriousness—the forward and severe judging of others. . . . He is not to be understood of judging by persons in authority, within the verge of their office, nor of private judging concerning facts that are notorious; but of judging persons' future state, or the secret springs and principles of their actions, or about facts doubtful in themselves. To judge in these cases, and give decisive sentence, is to assume the seat of God and challenge his prerogative. Note, how bold a sinner is the forward and severe censurer! How ill-timed and arrogant are his censures! But there is one who will judge the censurer, and those he censures, without prejudice, passion, or partiality. And there is a time coming when men cannot fail judging aright concerning themselves and others, but following his judgment. This should make them now cautious of judging others, and careful in judging themselves.[3]

Questions for Discussion and Application

1. How does this chapter define the sin of judging? After reviewing the definition, put it in your own words.
2. Give some examples of premature or inaccurate judgments you have made yourself, or seen others make.
3. What do you think about this statement: "We have sins in places where we don't even know we have places"?
4. As you were reading this chapter, did you think of some sinful judgments you have made about other people, especially other Christians? If so, ask the Lord to forgive you and help you to stop "passing judgment" in that way. Also ask forgiveness from the people you have judged wrongly, if it has broken or weakened your relationship with them.

CHAPTER TWO

Judgment Day

I n his case against judging in 1 Corinthians 4:3–5, the apostle Paul has called two witnesses so far—the incompleteness of man's judgment (it is seriously limited) and the insubordination of man's judgment (it is a sin of disobedience to God). In verse 5 he calls another witness—the *inappropriateness* of judging. The kind of judgment he is discussing is not appropriate for Christians, because a significant event has yet to occur that will render all such human judgment unnecessary.

Paul says, "Therefore do not go on passing judgment *before the time.*" The Greek phrase translated "before the time" (*pro kairou*, lit. "before time") could be a colloquial phrase meaning "ahead of time," "too early," or "prematurely." But it is most likely a reference to "the appointed time" (NIV) when Jesus Christ returns to the world, as is suggested by the next part of the verse, which says, "but wait until the Lord comes." That future court date, which Paul had described in the previous chapter (1 Cor. 3:10–15), is the *only* appropriate time for some judgments, because the Judge will be present, the evidence will all be clearly laid out, and a truly righteous verdict will be handed down.

If we make judgments now, on matters we are not qualified to judge, we are like a man who gets a jury notice in the mail, then sits down in his lazy-boy to read it. It says that on a certain date he will appear in court to judge the case of a man accused of child abuse. And there in his recliner, the man slaps his knee in anger and says, "I can't believe this guy did that to his kids—I hope they lock him up for life!" Even though he is missing many important facts about the case, even though his knowledge is embarrassingly limited, and long before the court has even convened, he has already passed sentence in his mind! Before you go on thinking how inexcusable that would be, however, realize that you are essentially doing the same thing when you judge others "before the time." That is the point Paul is trying to get across when he refers to the Second Coming of Christ in this passage. He believes that a better understanding of the only appropriate Judgment Day will help us to obey the command that he has just given.

The Return of the Judge

First Corinthians 4:5 says, "Therefore do not go on passing judgment before the time, but wait until the Lord comes." Judgments about some matters cannot and should not take place now, because the Judge is not physically present, but one day He will return and then the proper judgment will take place.

Who is the Judge? Clearly Paul is referring to Jesus Christ. The Bible repeatedly says that He has been appointed as the Judge of all mankind (Acts 10:42; 17:31; Rom. 2:16; 2 Tim. 4:1), and it also refers to Him repeatedly as the One who is coming (1 Cor. 15:23; 1 Thess. 2:19; 2 Thess. 2:1; Rev. 22:7, 12, 20). So when Paul says, "Wait until the Lord comes," he is speaking of the Second Coming of Christ. And the point that he wants to make clear, in relation to his case against judging, is that Jesus Christ is the only One fully *qualified* to judge some things and the only One fully *capable* of judging some things.

Jesus Christ is the only qualified Judge. The Greek word for "Lord" is *kyrios*, which speaks of both the deity and authority of Christ. It is a term that was used in the Septuagint, the Greek translation of the Old Testament, to refer to Jehovah, the Creator and God of Israel. The word also contains the idea of "master" (see Matt. 6:24), which implies that Jesus has been appointed to be the King and Ruler of His people, and one day the whole world. And in ancient times, of course, the king was the ultimate authority in all matters of legal judgment—he was the final arbiter of all questions and disputes. So Jesus Christ is the Lord and Judge, and we all are merely His servants. We must remember this distinction if we are to avoid the damaging and divisive sin of judging.

Romans 14:4 asks, "Who are you to judge the servant of another? To his own master he stands or falls; and he will stand, for the Lord is able to make him stand." An employee is in no position to sit in judgment on another employee—even a boss in one company has no right to judge an employee of another one. An employee answers only to his own boss, a slave is accountable only to his own master, and a servant can be judged only by his Lord. Jesus Christ is qualified to judge us because He is the Lord.

Jesus Christ is the only capable Judge. Jesus is the only One who can "know all things" (John 21:17). He is the eternal Word of God (John 1:1) who alone is "able to judge the thoughts and intentions of the heart" (Heb. 4:12). We as human beings, on the other hand, are not capable of acquiring and retaining all the details of any particular situation, nor are we able to discern what is inside the hearts of others. That is why Paul says, "Wait until the Lord comes." Only when the Divine Judge is present can a fair trial take place.

The Revelation of the Facts

First Corinthians 4:5 says, "Therefore do not go on passing judgment before the time, but wait until the Lord comes who will both bring to light the things hidden in the darkness and disclose the motives of men's hearts." There is no case in any trial without facts, and any verdict that is reached before the Lord comes is invalid, because too much critical evidence is missing. And in this verse, Paul tells us about the most important missing evidence in any spiritual judgment.

What the Lord will do when He returns is described by two Greek verbs (*phōtisei* and *phanerōsei*) that could both be translated by the English word "reveal." So Paul is saying that the last day will be a day of revelation, and the facts that will be revealed are "the things hidden in the darkness" and "the motives of men's hearts." In these words we learn not only what will be made known when Christ comes back, but also what we are not allowed to judge in the time prior to His coming.

Remember that Paul commands us not to judge others in this verse, but in other verses, even in the same book of 1 Corinthians, he says that we *should* judge others. For instance, in 5:12 he says that the church should "judge those who are within the church" in matters of church discipline. And in a similar vein, 6:5 says that we should be able to "decide between [our] brethren" and avoid secular lawsuits. The same could be said of Jesus and James, who issued the commands "Do not judge" (Matt. 7:1–2; James 4:12), but at other times encouraged us to do so (Matt.

7:15–16; James 5:19–20). So evaluating other Christians and reaching a conclusion about their conduct, even a negative one, is not necessarily wrong. In fact, Christian life and ministry require that we constantly discern, or judge, the rightness or wrongness of what is said and done by other believers (Matt. 18:15–17; 1 Thess. 5:21–22). A whole book could be written about how we *should* judge! In fact, some good books like that have indeed been written, including one by Erwin Lutzer, entitled *Who Are You to Judge?*[1] The message of that book might seem contradictory to the message of this one, but it actually is complementary, because the Bible does teach that we should judge right from wrong, and discern truth from error.

So the meaning of all those commands against judging, and the answer to these apparent contradictions, must lie in the issue of what is being judged. The Bible teaches that there are some things about others that we can and should judge, and that there are some other things that we cannot and should not judge. What we cannot and should not judge is described for us in the verse we are studying.

"The things hidden in the darkness." The literal wording of this phrase is "the hidden things of darkness," as the King James Version translates it. But what does it mean? Some commentators say that this is merely the first part of a parallelism—in other words, this phrase has the same meaning as "the motives of men's hearts." But this is unlikely, because of the double use of the Greek conjunction *kai* (translated "both/and"). Also, if Paul had meant it in this way, he would probably have used other language, such as "the thoughts hidden in darkness." Some other commentators recognize a distinction between the two phrases—they think Paul was referring to deeds in the first and thoughts in the second. But again,

Paul could have said "deeds" if he meant deeds, but he did not use that word.

The language that is used emphasizes the idea that some things have not been revealed yet, but will be one day. And since the next verse contains a clear reference to the Bible, I believe that Paul is referring here *to what the Bible does not tell us.*[2] He is saying that when Christ comes, He will reveal the unrevealed, unveiling many new truths and answering many questions that the Bible does not address. Until then, we need to leave those matters to the mind of God, and not make judgments about "the things hidden in the darkness."[3]

Since I raised the issue of drinking alcohol in chapter 1, I will use it as an example at this point, though not without some trepidation. I am afraid that I will lose those readers who are against drinking early in the book, and that those who enjoy it will think that this is so obvious that they can skip this part. But please keep an open mind if you are in the first group, and if you are in the second group, keep in mind that this is just one example, and what we discuss here will apply to other areas in your life.

The Bible says a lot about the consumption of alcohol, but never says that it is a sin to drink. We are told, "Do not get drunk with wine" (Eph. 5:18), we are warned about its addictive and destructive properties (Prov. 23:29–35), and perhaps even encouraged to consider abstinence as a legitimate lifestyle choice, at least for some people (e.g., the Old Testament priests, Samson, and John the Baptist). But nowhere do we read that it is wrong to partake, as long as we do not become inebriated to the point where we are no longer "filled with the Spirit" (Eph. 5:18 again) as evidenced by the fruit of the Spirit, which includes self-control (Gal. 5:23). In fact, Jesus Himself drank wine (Luke

7:34), and He even *made wine* from water at the wedding feast in Cana, which was His first miracle (John 2:1–11).

I know that various attempts have been made to support abstinence as a universal moral standard, but they are frankly too weak to deserve serious consideration. Some say that the wine that Jesus and other Christians drank in Bible times was watered down so much that it was more like grape juice. Besides being questionable historically, this idea simply cannot explain why Paul told the Ephesians not to get drunk with wine, if they would have had to drink gallons of it to do so! That command certainly implies that it was possible to get drunk on the wine of the day, and even implies that it was relatively easy. Other arguments are just as unstable—an unbiased reading of Scripture indicates that drinking alcohol in moderation is acceptable to God.[4]

Yet some Christians judge others in this regard. They think that those who drink are sinning, or perhaps they assume that someone who does so is not spiritual enough to be a church leader. Either way, they are making a judgment based on a nonbiblical or extrabiblical standard. They have gone farther than the Scriptures go in their evaluation of others. There is nothing wrong with a particular Christian choosing to abstain from alcohol, of course— we have the liberty to hold and live out our own convictions in areas like this, as Paul says in Romans 14:1–5. But we must be careful not to violate the liberty of others by judging them for their own personal choices, as that same passage also teaches (vv. 4, 13).

We will discuss Romans 14 more extensively in chapter 8, but for now let me say that any moral issue not addressed in the Bible can be inserted into that passage (and into 1 Cor. 8 also)—including all of the issues that I mentioned in the introduction to this book. In those sections of Scripture, Paul is teaching about "the things hidden in the darkness," using meat offered to idols as his primary example. And his consistent message is that issues like that have been left in the darkness for a reason—God wanted to allow freedom for different Christians to make different choices in those areas, without being judged by other believers.

So in 1 Corinthians 4:5 Paul says that "the things hidden in the darkness" will be revealed at the final judgment, but until then they will remain hidden, and they cannot be used as a basis for any human judgments now.

"The motives of men's hearts." What will be disclosed at the last day is not only the things outside of Scripture that have not been revealed, but also the things *inside* of each man that only God can see. The Greek word translated "motives" is *boulē*, which primarily refers to the intentions behind our actions, but also encompasses the thoughts and desires that contribute to the plans we formulate in our minds. So basically everything that goes on inside of us will be made known, or exposed, when the Lord comes.

Knowing that fact is both frightening and comforting, isn't it? It is frightening because we have so many thoughts, desires, and intentions that are less than laudable—in fact, many are downright disgusting. Consequently, we should allow this truth about the Second Coming to sink into our hearts and change our lives. The Stoic philosopher Seneca seemed to understand this idea when he wrote: "I will govern my life and my thoughts as if the whole world were to see the one, and to read the other. For what does it signify to make anything a secret to our neighbor, when to God, who is the Searcher of hearts, all our privacies are open"? [5] This also has special reference to those who judge others, because sinful judgments, even when they are made only in our minds, will be revealed at the last day. God knows when we are wrongfully judging one another, and apparently everyone else will too.

But it is also comforting to know that Jesus will "disclose the motives of men's hearts" when He returns, because, by the grace of God working in us, we Christians have many good motives for what we do. And even though people may misunderstand and misjudge what is inside our hearts, God never will. He knows the truth, and He will reward us one day for the good intentions of our heart. That is the thrust of this particular passage, because Paul goes on to say, "Then each man's praise will come to him from God." Before discussing that part of the passage, however, I want to give a few more examples of sinful judging, which illustrate both of the areas we are not supposed to judge.

I have always been tempted to judge people who have a lot of money (maybe because I have never had much myself!). While attending a conference a few years ago, I stayed with a couple who had a new house that was so big my entire house would have fit in half of the third floor! The man was an elder at the host church, but I confess that when I first arrived I concluded that he could not be very spiritual, and that the only reason he was a leader in the church was his financial resources. But as I got to know him, I found out more information, such as the fact that his former house had burned to the ground a few years before, and he was actually somewhat embarrassed about how big the replacement ended up being. I also found out through others that this house in this area was actually modest, considering his salary. And finally, he was extremely generous with the church and with the poor, giving a large percentage of his income to both.

I was reminded by a friend that the Bible never says it is wrong to be rich—only that those who are rich should not love their possessions too much and should be ready to share them (1 Tim. 6:17–19). In my mind I had taken the scriptural principle of *not loving money* and extended it to the non-scriptural idea of *not having money.* So in my moral judgments I had gone "beyond what is written." I also had judged this man's heart, assuming that he must have loved his money more than God. It has been necessary for me to repent of this sin, and guard my mind against it in similar situations.

Sometimes sinful judging can be modeled by the leadership of a church, which will then create a judgmental atmosphere among the body. A letter I once received provides an example of this:

> Our denomination believes in having revival services, which run for one week, twice a year. My husband and I do not object to having the revival services; however, we are having great difficulty resolving the issue of whether or not we, as a family, should attend every single service held during that week. Prior to every revival we have, for about 2–3 weeks the Pastor's messages revolve around our "obligation" to be at the revival services. These get so heavy to the point of implying that if you do not attend every service, then you must be backslidden, or nearly so, and your priorities are messed up, because you do not *want* to be at church, attending an opportunity to worship the Lord, and learning from His Word.
>
> However, my husband feels that we have a responsibility to our family given by God, and that it is not right to force us to keep our children up past 9:00 P.M. when they have school the next day, especially for an entire week. He is not opposed to going to some of the services, or even having one of us go, while the other stays home with the

children. Our pastor has two young children also, and has said that he believes they should be in church, regardless of school, because God comes first. He has also said that you will be where you *want* to be, and if you truly want to be in church, in the presence of God, then you will be. Again this implies that if you are not there, then you must not want to be, so you must not love the Lord like you should.

This is an example of what we could call legalism, the institutional and instructional form of judging, which we will discuss later in the book. Notice how this pastor, and undoubtedly other people in the church, have gone "beyond what is written." The Bible says that we should not be "forsaking the assembling of ourselves together" (Heb. 10:25, KJV), but it does not say we have to attend church every time the doors are open. The atmosphere in that woman's church is also judgmental in regard to heart issues, because of the clear implications that are being made about the motives of those who do not attend every service. So even though that pastor's teaching is filled with biblical references and pious sentiment, its fruit will be confusion in the hearts of good people who love the Lord, and division between those with different practices.[6]

That pastor, and the people in the church, cannot know whether those who miss some of the meetings are right or wrong. That issue is outside of Scripture and depends too much on the thoughts and intentions of the heart, so judgment should be withheld until the Judge returns and all the facts are revealed.

The Reception of the Verdict

First Corinthians 4:5 concludes by saying, "And then each man's praise will come to him from God." In the

Greek text, the word translated "praise" is in an emphatic position. It is noteworthy that Paul chooses to emphasize that Christians will receive a positive commendation when the Judge returns. He does not mention the guilty verdict that unbelievers will receive on that day, but he wants us to know that when the Lord comes, many believers will hear Him say, "Well done, thou good and faithful servant" (Matt. 25:21, KJV).

Why does Paul choose to mention the reception of a positive verdict? He is probably thinking of the conflicts in the church that he had addressed in 1 Corinthians 3, the previous chapter, where factions were gathering against Paul in support of Apollos, and vice versa. In other words, the two men were being judged by those who opposed them. So here Paul says that *both* he and Apollos will receive praise from God at the last day. And as verse 6 adds, he is merely using himself and Apollos as an illustration, so what he says applies to every faithful believer who has been judged unfairly by others.

When you find yourself reaching a negative conclusion in your mind about another Christian, remember this: when the Lord returns, if it is made clear that there was freedom on that issue and his motives were right, that person *will* receive praise from God, whether you think he should get it or not. Romans 14:2–4 makes the same point:

> One person has faith that he may eat all things, but he who is weak eats vegetables only. The one who eats is not to regard with contempt the one who does not eat, and the one who does not eat is not to judge the one who eats, for God has accepted him. Who are you to judge the servant of another? To his own master he stands or falls; and he will stand, for the Lord is able to make him stand.

So Paul's point at the end of 1 Corinthians 4:5 is that when the verdict is handed down at the future Judgment Day, all those who have been wrongly judged by others will be vindicated and rewarded by God Himself. I don't know about you, but I don't want to be the fool who passed judgment on them before the time. I don't want to stand under the fiery glare of our holy God, and hear Him say to me, "Did you think that this child of mine was wrong in what he did, and criticize him to others?"

"Y-y-yes, Lord," I will have to answer, with a gulp.

"Well, I did not think he was wrong at all! Nothing in My Bible said what he did was wrong, and I happen to know that his heart was right, which makes Me quite pleased with him. So the only person who was wrong in that situation was you!"

I know that the Lord Jesus died for my sins, even my sins of judging, and that I will be forgiven through faith in Him. But I still do not want to find out that I have wronged my brothers and sisters in this way, and caused unnecessary division or distance between myself and them. By God's grace I want to avoid such judgment until the day when the true Judge returns, the full facts are revealed, and the just verdict is received.

Questions for Discussion and Application

1. Why is Jesus Christ the only human being who is fully qualified and able to judge other humans?
2. Why do you think that God has left many of our lifestyle choices "hidden in the darkness"? Why did He not give us a rule book that covers everything we might do?

3. Can you think of an example where you were sure of someone else's thoughts or motives, only to find out they were very different from what you thought?
4. As a case study, how would you counsel the woman who wrote the letter about "revival services" (pp. 26–27)?

Cross-Examining
Your Judgments

I can't believe you would do such a thing! I could never do that. . . ."

"I don't believe that for a minute. I know what you're really thinking."

How do you feel when people say things like that to you, implying that their preferences are superior to yours, or that they know your heart better than you do? It probably makes you feel angry, or at least keeps you from wanting to fellowship with them. That is one reason why judging is such a dangerous and damaging sin—it builds major barriers between people. To put it another way, we become severely tempted to sin when we are judged by others, especially when they are wrong about us. Our Satanic enemy and our sinful flesh revel in such an opportunity to cause us to become bitter at our critics, judge them in return, or strike back at them for the injustice they have done to us. When sinful judging takes place, the wall goes up, and the gap between people just widens from there, developing into full-blown hostility (or deep-seated prejudice between whole groups of people).[1]

Another reason that the sin of judging is so significant is that it happens inside our hearts and minds, out of which all our words and actions flow (Prov. 4:23; Rom. 12:2). And because it happens inside our hearts and minds, it is often the *first* sin that we commit in a progression of sin that leads to serious trouble in our relationships with others. So if we can learn to recognize and repent of this sin, we can stop that ill-fated journey before it starts and get off the road to ruin.

To do that, we have to learn to guard our hearts and be renewed in our minds (Prov. 4:23 and Rom. 12:2 again). We have to fight the spiritual battle at the level of our thinking, "taking every thought captive to the obedience of Christ" (2 Cor. 10:5). We have to put off the old ways of thinking and put on the new ways (Eph. 4:22–24), and learn to focus on what is true and right (Phil. 4:8) rather than making judgments about others that are false and wrong. So to help you learn and practice these spiritual skills, I want to suggest five questions that you should ask yourself whenever you find yourself forming a negative opinion about another person. If you constantly cross-examine your judgments with these questions, you will not so often be found guilty by God for the sin of judging.

Is this opinion based firmly on Scripture, or on my ideas and preferences?

First Corinthians 4:5 says that we should not judge "the things hidden in the darkness," and the next verse says we should not "exceed what is written." As long as our steps are falling within the landscape of Scripture, we are safe in our judgments about others. But as we get close to the edge of what the Bible addresses, we must be careful not to walk off the cliff into the air of sinful judging. In other words, we can go as far as the Word goes, but no further.

Is the person saying or doing something that the Scripture forbids? Do you have a verse, or preferably more than one, that proves he or she is wrong? If not, you may want to ask the person questions, or even ask others about it (without mentioning the person's name)—but you should withhold judgment at this time. And even if you do believe that he or she is violating Scripture in some way, you should still realize that you could be wrong about what the Scripture says. That is one reason why Jesus instituted the process of church discipline, or loving confrontation (as I prefer to call it), in Matthew 18:15–17. In that passage our Lord says to tell the other Christian why you think he is wrong, and then if he does not agree, take one or two others with you. That way if you are misunderstanding or misapplying the Scriptures in the situation, you can be corrected.

I have seen many Christians judge others on matters not addressed in the Bible (I have done so myself too many times), and I also have seen them misinterpret and misuse the Scriptures, because they wanted to impose their preference on others. This practice is pandemic in the church, but let me share a few examples of it.

Different styles of music. I have never found a single passage in the Bible that was given for the purpose of addressing the style of music that we listen to, or use in corporate worship. Nevertheless, Christians are constantly judging one another on this issue, and even twisting and stretching the Scriptures to support their particular preference. I once heard a preacher use 1 Peter 2:8, "the rock that makes men stumble," to say that modern music styles will cause us to sin. The verse has nothing to do with music at all, of course—it is about the person and work of Christ.

I have heard someone else say that churches who sing only old hymns are displeasing to the Lord because the Psalms say we should sing a "new song" unto Him. But those references in Psalms are primarily metaphorical, meaning that our singing, and every part of our lives, should be different than our old sinful selves and the godless tradition of the world around us. Further, the Bible contains examples of the people of God singing old music, including the Psalms themselves, which continued to be sung for many generations after they were written.

Those are extreme cases of judging in regard to music styles, but there are others that are more subtle and influential. People who like contemporary music can sometimes make very negative judgments about those who do not prefer it, such as concluding that they are not concerned for evangelism and church growth. Or we may assume that such people are judgmental and legalistic if they cringe at drums in the worship service, when it may be that they just find certain instruments unpleasant. How's that for subtle—judging that someone else is judging?! But it is possible and it happens.

On the other hand, the arguments used against contemporary music can sometimes exhibit award-worthy creativity. Some say that if the rhythm in music is emphasized more than the melody and harmony, it is ungodly. Another argument is that some types of music are acceptable to God because of where the primary beat falls, but others are not acceptable because the primary beat falls somewhere else.[2] These ideas do not arise from the exegesis of Scripture, to say the least, and upon closer inspection are actually *inconsistent* with Scripture. When we take into account the types of instruments that were used in Old Testament worship, which included tambourines, cymbals, and the guitar-like lyres and lutes (Pss. 68:24–25; 98:4–6; 149:3; 150:1–6), it is likely that the music of the Jews was quite heavy in the rhythm department. And given the lack of professional composition in most cases, the beat was probably falling all over the place!

Many Christians are critical of other churches (and perhaps sometimes their own) because of the use of modern praise choruses in the worship services. They assume something must be wrong with the raising of hands during singing, and they say things like, "The mindless repetition in that happy-clappy church impoverishes the people of God," and "these people wouldn't know true worship if it hit them on their lolling heads." But this is an example of going beyond what is written, because the Scriptures mention the lifting of hands and clapping in the context of corporate worship (Ps. 63:4; 1 Tim. 2:8; Ps. 47:1), and the inspired lyrics of the psalmist are often simple and repetitive (Pss. 117, 134, 136). I do not believe we are *commanded* to do these things in our worship (my church is actually more traditional in this regard), but we are certainly *allowed* to practice them. So it is wrong to state or imply that God is displeased with a church simply because it has a contemporary style of worship.[3]

On the other hand, it is not sinful judging to demand that the words of the songs be consistently biblical. Jesus said that we are to worship Him "in spirit and in truth," so we can say it is wrong to sing lyrics that are contrary to His Word. We should indeed make judgments about music, or any other element of worship, when we have clear scriptural reasons to do so. And in those cases, no one can rightly accuse us of being judgmental. We are merely obeying 1 Thessalonians 5:21–22, which says we should "examine everything carefully; hold fast to that which is good; abstain from every form of evil."

Women working. Here is another example of how Christians often cross the line between acceptable and sinful judgments. In the introduction to this book, I included the statement, "Any woman who works a full-time job is neglecting her children." That statement crosses the line into sinful judging because it implies that every woman who works full-time is necessarily grieving God by doing so. But it is conceivable that some women can have a job and not neglect their children (especially if they have a lot of good help). And if they are not neglecting their family, they are not grieving God, because although He said women should be workers at home (Titus 2:4), He never said they could not work outside the home also (see Prov. 31:10–16). So we cannot judge a particular woman simply because she works full-time outside the home. We would have to find out whether she is fulfilling the biblical commands to teach and discipline her children (Deut. 6:7; Prov. 23:13–14), and whether she is able to accomplish the work she needs to do in the home (Titus 2:4 and Prov. 31 again).

On the other hand, it is not judgmental to encourage such women, and their husbands, to examine this issue carefully, because working outside the home can often result in neglect of the children. And it would not be wrong to conclude that a particular working mother should not be working so much, when there is evidence that the clear commands of Scripture are not being fulfilled. Again, the process that Jesus mentions in Matthew 18:16 of taking "one or two more," and even seeking counsel from the leaders of the church, can help bring about clarity in situations like this.

Birth control. This final example is related to women and children as well. Many Christians believe and teach that it is a sin to use any form of birth control—that God wants us to have as many children as we possibly can. The Bible contains no command against birth control, so to make their case they must support it from passages of Scripture that simply do not say as much as they want them to say.

"Be fruitful and multiply" (Gen. 1:22, 28), if it applies directly to us today,[4] may mean that a married couple should have children, but it does not specify *how many* children they should have. "Children are a gift of the LORD. . . . How blessed is the man whose quiver is full of them" (Ps. 127:3–5) gives us good reason to have children, and even to have more than we might otherwise have. But again, it does not tell us how many we must have, or that we can never take a break from having them. And the fact that the Lord opens and closes the womb (Gen. 29:31; 1 Sam. 1:5) does not necessarily mean that couples who use birth control are not trusting in God, as some allege. It means that God is in providential control over all that happens, but we must remember that He uses *our choices* as a means to His providential ends. In other words, trusting God does not prevent us from making choices or exercising control in those areas of our lives where He has allowed us freedom.[5] I can trust God that He will provide for me in case of emergency, for example, but still purchase an insurance policy, believing that He will provide for me *through* the choice I have made and the planning I have done.

We could discuss each of these examples in much more depth, of course, but hopefully these brief words about them will challenge you to make sure your judgments about others are based firmly on Scripture, and not just on your own ideas and preferences.

Does the formation of this opinion include any judgments about the person's thoughts or motives?

First Corinthians 4:5 also says that we should not judge "the motives of men's hearts." We should withhold judgment not only on that which is outside of Scripture, but also on that which is inside of man. We simply cannot know for sure what people are thinking or desiring, unless they tell us. As long as their thoughts and intentions remain in their hearts, only God can judge such matters (Jer. 17:9–10). As 1 Samuel 16:7 says, "God sees not as man sees, for man looks at the outward appearance, but the Lord looks at the heart."

We are so prone to assume that we know what others are thinking, especially when there are outward evidences that seem to be pointing toward our conclusion. But we must realize that things are not always what they seem, particularly when it comes to this complex organism known as *homo sapiens*. Someone may use certain words that I would use only with bad intentions, but he might mean something totally different by them. You might be convinced that the look on your friend's face indicates disgust directed toward you, but it could merely be the result of some bad pizza she had for lunch! And we might assume that others are trying to deceive us, when they themselves actually have the wrong information, or are simply not remembering correctly. Their motives may be right, even when what they say is wrong.

That last statement applies even to theological differences between believers—an issue that is often the occasion for sinful judgments. We can and should judge what people say about their beliefs, whether it is consistent with the Bible or not. But we must be very careful not to ascribe bad motives to them. For instance, as a Reformed Christian I find it easy to assume certain things about the hearts of those who are not Reformed in their doctrine. I tend to think that they are not willing to study enough to get to the truth, that they are afraid of the unpopularity that true doctrine brings, or even that they want to believe that they have contributed to their salvation, and are really trusting in their own works rather than in Christ. But although some of those things might be true of some non-Reformed people, it simply does not follow for all of them. It is possible that they have studied more than I have, but come to different conclusions. They may be genuinely open and willing to embrace whatever God says in His Word, but simply haven't been "enlightened" to my particular view yet (in other words, God has sovereignly ordained that they would be Arminians at this time!). And to say that non-Reformed persons are trusting in their own works, even when they loudly proclaim that they trust in Christ alone, is the epitome of a sinful judgment. You could say that such a person's doctrine is inconsistent with his profession, but you should never call him a liar.

In fact, I have personally known some non-Reformed believers (even fully Arminian ones) who seem to have *good motives* for their rejection of Calvinism. What I mean is that they love Christ, and because of bad experiences with Reformed teaching (or bad Reformed teachers), they fear that our theology makes God look bad, or impugns His justice and sincerity. Though I do not agree with this concern, I can certainly understand where it comes from, and how good-hearted people could be put off by the doctrines I hold dear. So though I may judge their theological articulations to be in error, I do not need to assume or imply that their motives are wrong.[6]

Even when you are evaluating someone's actions, which is a legitimate practice, be careful not to allow opinions or implications about motives to creep in as well. For instance, you may say someone is being "manipulative" or "controlling" because of a real behavior problem you see in a particular situation. But notice that those words necessarily imply something about the motives behind the person's actions. If there was no real intent to manipulate or control the situation—if there was some other reason for what was done . . . up goes the wall between you and that individual, because you are misjudging motives! Another example would be if I had an assistant pastor under me who differed with me doctrinally, and led some people out of the church, and I called him an Absalom (see 2 Sam. 15). I would be going farther than just saying his actions were wrong or unwise—I would be clearly implying that his motives were to usurp my authority, because that is what Absalom tried to do. But the situation may be much more complex than a mere power-play, and addressing it that way would only exacerbate the problem.

One more example should suffice for this part of the discussion. In my introduction I included the statement, "People who take Prozac and other psychiatric medications are not trusting God." This is a judgment that I myself have made in the past, because I am extremely skeptical about the conventional wisdom in the medical field regarding psychological problems and their solutions. I still have that skepticism—in fact, it only seems to deepen with my further research on the issue and my experience as a counselor.[7] But I have backed off from my former judgment, simply because I do not know the heart of every person who takes psychiatric medications. I have come to recognize that some people probably take them *because* they are trusting God, and think this is the help that God has provided for them. I may disagree with their perspective on the problem and the solution, but I must be careful not to ascribe wrong motives to them, unless they tell me about motives that are contrary to Scripture. If as a pastor and counselor I automatically assume that it is a sin for people to take those kinds of drugs, I will cut myself off from them before I have a chance to help them. I also run the risk of fostering an overemphasis on the outward, physical issue of medication, when my ministry to them should be primarily concerned with the inward, spiritual issues of the heart.

Am I missing any facts that are necessary for an accurate evaluation?

"He who gives an answer before he hears," Proverbs 18:13 says, "it is folly and shame to him." And Proverbs 18:17 warns us, "The first to plead his case seems right, until another comes and examines him." Many sinful judgments proceed from nothing more than a lack of all the facts. The following story illustrates this well:

You haven't seen your friend Jane for several months; she's been away traveling. This morning you see her at church, seated on the opposite side of the building. You can't wait till the service is over to talk to her. At the conclusion of the service, you rush around the pews and happily call to her, "Jane! Jane! It's so good to see you!" But Jane sticks her nose into the air, turns on her heel, and sails out of the church as rapidly as possible, without so much as a "how do you do?"

You stand there hurt and perplexed. If you respond as many do, you'll say, "Hurrrruuummmph! If that's the way she's going to act, then so be it! I can wait till she comes down off her high horse and wants to talk. Then maybe I'll be ready to do so and maybe I won't!"

But, you see, Jesus won't let you do that. He tells you to go after her. . . . Suppose you do. Having recovered from the shock, you say to yourself, "Something's wrong here. I've got to get to the bottom of it. I can't have this happen to Jane and me." So you hightail it out of the church after her. There she is over at her car. You go over and you say, "Jane! What's wrong? I was so glad to see you home again that I rushed over to see you after church, but when I called to you, you stuck your nose in the air and left. What's wrong?"

Perhaps Jane's response will be something like this: "Oh no! Mary, I didn't even hear or see you! You see, I caught a bad cold on my trip abroad, and the pastor preached forever, and I left my tissues in the car, and I thought for sure I was going to drip all over my new dress and my Bible. That's why I put my nose back and rushed out here to get those tissues. I was so preoccupied with all that I didn't see or hear you."[8]

How easy it would have been for the one woman to trust her own powers of observation enough to form an opinion about the other! But she would have been wrong, and a totally unnecessary wall would have gone up between them that would have grown with the next potential misunderstanding, and the next, until it became an almost impenetrable barrier. So to keep that from happening, keep in mind what Jesus said in John 7:24: "Do not judge according to appearance, but judge with righteous judgment."

Imagine this fictional conversation between a crying woman and her new pastor, who run into each other outside the doctor's office:

"What's wrong, sister?"

"Oh, pastor, I can't live with my husband right now, or even be close to him—"

"Oh sister, that's no way out of your problems! The Word of God says, 'Whatsoever God has joined together, let no man put asunder!' We need to get you into counseling and keep you from doing this thing that will ruin your life and your relationship with God."

"No, pastor—I can't live with my husband right now, or be close to him, because of a contagious disease—"

"Oh well, that's different. Why didn't you say so? We'll get some medical help for your husband, and you just move right in with my wife and me. We'll take care of you, and we won't take no for an answer, even though you might feel embarrassed and not want to put us out. We absolutely insist—oh, I feel so sorry for you!"

Before the older woman can stop him, the well-meaning young pastor gives her a big long hug.

"No, pastor, I can't live with my husband right now, or even be close to him, because of a contagious disease *that I have.*"

Wouldn't that encounter have gone so much better if the pastor had just listened more, instead of having his mouth in gear and his brain in neutral? Likewise, all our relationships would be so much better if we always made sure to get all the facts before making a judgment about others.

How would I want this person to think of me if the roles were reversed?

Would you like it if, without any biblical basis, someone concluded that you were sinning? Would you want someone to make judgments about your motives, even when you are saying the opposite, and thus imply a better knowledge of you than you have of yourself? Should someone form a negative opinion of you in a particular situation before having all the facts? On the contrary, wouldn't you want that other person to be careful to withhold judgment until he or she has heard your side, and listen sympathetically to what you have to say? Well, Jesus said that you should treat others as you would want to be treated (Matt. 7:12; Luke 6:31).

This principle has been aptly called the Golden Rule, and it is truly the most valuable key to good relationships, especially in regard to the judgments we make about others. To follow the Golden Rule requires the practice of another principle that I call the "Shoes Principle." To know how you would want to be treated if you were someone else means that you have to put yourself in his or her shoes. You have to imagine yourself in such a position, and think of what would be best for you if the roles were reversed.

The interesting irony about the Golden Rule, which provides motivation for us to apply it, is that the way we treat others is often the way we end up being treated! Consider the words of Christ in Matthew 7:1–2: "Do not judge so that you will not be judged. For in the way you judge, you will be judged; and by your standard of measure, it will be measured to you."

This reminds me of a scene in Shakespeare's *Henry V*, where the young king has learned of a plot to assassinate him by three of his officers—Scroop, Cambridge, and Grey. Henry calls for a conference with the three traitors. While they are still unaware that the king knows of their crime, he gives an order to release a prisoner who had earlier been arrested for treason.

"That's mercy, but too much security," Scroop objects. "Let him be punished, sovereign, lest his example breed, by his sufferance, more of such a kind."

"O, let us yet be merciful," Henry replies. But the other two traitors, Cambridge and Grey, chime in with their objections to Henry's inclination. So Henry hands them papers, which they think are orders, but when they start reading them, they soon see that the papers chronicle their own treason against the king.

"Why, how now, gentlemen!" Henry says. "What see you in those papers that you lose so much complexion? Look ye, how they change! Their cheeks are paper. Why, what read you there, that have so cowarded and chased your blood out of appearance?"

"I do confess my fault," Cambridge says. "And do submit me to your Highness' mercy."

"To which we all appeal," Grey and Scroop add together.

But King Henry answers, "The mercy that was quick in us but late, by your own counsel is suppressed and killed. You must not dare, for shame, to talk of mercy, for your own reasons turn into your bosoms, as dogs upon their masters, worrying you."

And the traitorous officers are sent away to be executed.[9]

In case you missed the point in all that Elizabethan English, those men were judged in the way that they had judged, and were measured by the same standard by which they measured others. The same thing will happen to you, if you are not careful to avoid sinful judgments and eager to think the best about others. You will find yourself under suspicion by others. On the other hand, if you are a loving person who "believes all things, hopes all things" about others (1 Cor. 13:7), you will find that others will be more likely to give you the benefit of the doubt as well.

How can I show the grace of the cross to this person?

The reason that you should want to believe the best about others, and give them the benefit of the doubt, is that God has been so gracious to you. Ephesians 4:32 says, "Be kind to one another, tender-hearted, forgiving each other, *just as God in Christ also has forgiven you.*" The Greek verb translated "forgiving" and "forgiven" in that verse (*charizō*) comes from the word for grace, so Paul is saying we should be gracious to others as God has been gracious to us. And how gracious has God been to us? Consider these verses:

> God demonstrates His own love toward us, in that while we were yet sinners, Christ died for us. . . . While we were enemies we were reconciled to God through the death of His Son. (Rom. 5:8–10)

> You were dead in your trespasses and sins, in which you formerly walked according to the course of this world, according to the prince of the power of the air, of the spirit that is now working in the sons of disobedience. Among them we too all formerly lived in the lusts of our flesh, indulging the desires of the flesh and of the mind, and were by nature children of wrath, even as the rest. But God, being rich in mercy, because of His great love with which He loved us, even when we were dead in our transgressions, made us alive together with Christ (by grace you have been saved). (Eph. 2:1–5)

> We also once were foolish ourselves, disobedient, deceived, enslaved to various lusts and pleasures, spending our life in malice and envy, hateful, hating one another. But when the kindness of God our Savior and His love for mankind appeared, He saved us, not on the basis of deeds which we have done in righteousness, but according to His mercy, by the washing of regeneration and renewing by the Holy Spirit, whom He poured out upon us richly through Jesus Christ our Savior, so that being justified by His grace we would be made heirs according to the hope of eternal life. (Titus 3:3–7)

Do you deserve all the good things God has given you, or the love and acceptance with which He looks upon you?

No, you don't even come close to deserving them. In fact, you deserve the opposite—an eternity in hell with His wrath poured out upon you. Yet Jesus bore the wrath of God for you and suffered the penalty of hell for you, so that God could forgive your sins and adopt you as His child, without compromising His justice. This is the grace of the cross. And this is the grace that the Lord wants you to show to others.

Do the people you are tempted to judge deserve your love and acceptance? Probably not, or you wouldn't be so tempted to judge them! But even if they are wrong in some way, and you need to help them to grow and mature in some way, this is the time they need grace from you, rather than condemnation and punishment. And as you believe the best about them and give them the benefit of the doubt, particularly in regard to their motives, you will be able to be used by God to bring healing to their hearts, and to their relationship with you. If you do not, you will only hurt them and yourself in the process.[10]

So before you open the next case, in which you will be evaluating another Christian, make an oath to the Divine Judge that you will base your conclusions on the truth, the whole truth, and nothing but the truth! And before you close the case by delivering a negative verdict about that other person, may you cross-examine your judgments with the five questions we have asked in this chapter and whatever others need to be asked. And when a particular thought has been exposed as a false witness, may you dismiss it summarily and replace it with thoughts that will lead you to the truth of the matter, because those good thoughts come from the Spirit of truth, are consistent with the Word of truth, and are centered on the One who is the Truth.

Questions for Discussion and Application

1. Have you been judged by others because of things that the Bible doesn't even talk about? Have you judged others in that way?
2. What does the fact that we tend to judge the thoughts and motives of others say about the importance of good communication?
3. The pastor in the story on pages 42–43 had "his mouth in gear and his brain in neutral." What are some practical ways you can avoid that problem?
4. Think about a conflict or difficulty you are having right now with another person. How could you apply the Golden Rule and the "Shoes Principle" in that situation?
5. What do you think about this statement: "A man who does not show grace to others has not experienced the grace of God himself."

Paul's Illustration
and Definition of Legalism

T he sin of judging is the individual and personal form of a problem that has been called legalism— or we could say that legalism is the institutional and doctrinal form of judging. Judging takes place between two people, while legalism is an approach to spirituality that permeates whole groups of people, because it is the result of a certain kind of teaching to which they are exposed.

In the passage we have been discussing, 1 Corinthians 4:3–7, the apostle Paul's progression of thought flows from the issue of certain Christians judging others to the idea that all Christians must learn to base their moral standards on the Scriptures alone. He writes, "Now these things, brethren, I have figuratively applied to myself and Apollos for your sakes, so that in us you may learn *not to exceed what is written*" (v. 6). In those words we find a biblical definition of legalism, which is sorely needed in the church today.

The Problem of Definition

As I mentioned in the introduction to this book, "legalism" is a term that is often thrown around, but not well understood or precisely defined.[1] It has widely different meanings to different people. For example, consider the following advertisement for a fundamentalist Bible college in the Midwest. At the top are a picture of the school's president, Dr. Jack Hyles, and another one of his mother, Mrs. C. M. Hyles. Underneath the pictures, the ad says this:

WAS MY MOTHER A LEGALIST WHEN SHE

Required me to go to church Sunday morning, Sunday night, and Wednesday night?

Required me to wear a tie to church? . . .

Taught me that such things as smoking, dancing, card-playing, movie-going and mixed bathing were wrong?

Refused to allow me to listen to suggestive and sensuous music?

Required me to go to the barber shop every two weeks? . . .

Of course she wasn't: She was showing her love for me.

Is Hyles-Anderson College legalistic because we follow Mama's teaching? *Of course we aren't: we simply love our students.* [2]

Jack Hyles's answer to whether his mother was legalistic is, "Of course she wasn't." And his answer to whether his college is legalistic is, "Of course we aren't." Yet many Christians would say, with all due respect to Jack's mama, that she was indeed legalistic, and so is the college that follows her teachings. So who is right? What is legalism, and what is not? Who is legalistic, and who is not?

One of the difficulties in answering this question is that "legalism" is a somewhat arbitrary word that lends itself to many definitions. The word itself is not found in the Bible, so we cannot do a word study to determine its meaning. Also, the word is used by Christians in connection with both justification and sanctification, two very different topics. When used in connection with justification, "legalism" usually means adding works to faith, or human merit to grace, as a condition for salvation. But when used in connection with sanctification (the Christian life after coming to salvation), the term usually has something to do with man-made traditions added to the Bible. Fundamentalists like Jack Hyles, who believe things like card-playing and movie-going are sinful, often answer the charge of legalism by saying that they believe in salvation by grace alone; therefore they are not legalists. They do not think the term applies to their rules and regulations for the Christian life.

However, 1 Corinthians 4 and many other biblical passages do apply to the standards by which we judge our own behavior and the behavior of other Christians. And that is the topic I will be discussing in the next few chapters. In the conclusion of this book I will discuss the idea of legalism in connection with salvation, but for now when I use the term, I will be referring to the error that Paul is addressing when he says, "Do not go beyond what is written." He is talking about the tendency of Christians to create moral standards that are not revealed in the Scriptures themselves, and to place those man-made standards on an equal level with the commands and principles of the Bible.

The Paul and Apollos Situation

When Paul says, "Now these things, brethren, I have figuratively applied to myself and Apollos" (1 Cor. 4:6), he is referring to what he has been discussing from the beginning of 1 Corinthians 3. The first mention of Paul and Apollos together is in verse 4 of that chapter: "For when one says, 'I am of Paul,' and another, 'I am of Apollos,' are you not mere men?" Then Paul goes on to address the factious spirit of the Corinthians, in which they were following one man to the exclusion of the other. They were elevating one man to a position of inordinate esteem, and putting down the other with critical and sinful judgments.

Consider these excerpts from the surrounding passages, so that you can understand the context of our passage better:

> I planted, Apollos watered, but God was causing the growth. So then neither the one who plants nor the one who waters is anything, but God who causes the growth. Now he who plants and he who waters are one; but each will receive his own reward according to his own labor. For we are God's fellow workers; you are God's field, God's building. According to the grace of God which was given to me, like a wise master builder I laid a foundation, and another is building on it. (1 Cor. 3:6–10)

> So then let no one boast in men. For all things belong to you, whether Paul or Apollos or Cephas or the world or life or death or things present or things to come; all things belong to you, and you belong to Christ; and Christ belongs to God. Let a man regard us in this manner, as servants of Christ and stewards of the mysteries of God. (1 Cor. 3:21–4:1)

This discussion of disunity in the body, where people were following one leader over the other, is the context in which Paul says, "But to me it is a very small thing that I may be examined by you, or by any human court" (1 Cor. 4:3). So it is clear that Paul was being judged by at least some of the Corinthians (if not the whole church). Apollos was apparently being judged also, by others. And some of the judgments being made about these men were based on extrabiblical standards, because Paul says that his point in discussing himself and Apollos is "that in us you may learn not to exceed what is written." So it might be helpful for us to consider what exactly was happening in this illustration of legalism that Paul provides for us. What issues were dividing the Corinthians?

One answer that seems likely, from the context, is that they were judging Paul and Apollos on the basis of how many converts they each had (see 1 Cor. 3:6–10). But, as Paul says in verse 2 of chapter 4, the most important factor in a man's ministry is not the number of converts he has (or how many people attend his church), but whether he is faithful to the Lord. Another basis for judgment may have been the way that the different men chose to go about their ministries, because Paul emphasizes that each minister will stand before the Lord, who alone can test the quality of his ministry (1 Cor. 3:10–15). But it seems very likely that the Corinthians were also judging Paul and Apollos on the basis of certain standards of conduct, which were highly disputed in the early church. We know from many other passages in Paul's writings that circumcision was such an issue (Gal. 2:3–4), along with eating meat offered to idols (1 Cor. 8) and the observation of the Sabbath Day (Rom. 14:5; Col. 2:16).

When you understand that in 1 Corinthians 4:6 Paul is saying, "I have used myself and Apollos above as an illustration" (Phillips translation), then it becomes apparent just how important his next words are. The point that Paul makes in the rest of the verse is the truth to which his whole discussion has been leading! More than a chapter of the Bible has been given primarily for the purpose of providing an illustration of this axiomatic principle: "Do not go beyond what is written."

Paul's *Sola Scriptura*

The apostle has been discussing himself and Apollos with the goal that the Corinthians, and all believers since them, might learn "not to exceed what is written." And not only is this principle the point of the whole preceding discussion, but it is also the cure for the dangers of spiritual pride and division among believers, as the rest of the passage indicates (see my discussion of these dangers in chapter 5).

The exact translation of this part of the verse poses some challenges,[3] as evidenced by the different renderings in the various Bible versions.[4] But the basic meaning is clear: Paul is warning us about the danger of drawing conclusions in our minds about matters not addressed in the Word of God. He uses the Greek word *gegraptai*, which means "things that have been written." It is a form of the term used more than any other in the New Testament to refer to the books of Scripture (or the Bible, as we call it today). The noun form (*graphē*) is used over fifty times to refer to the written Word, and the verb form (*graphō*) is used over a hundred times, often in the familiar phrase "It is written. . . ." So there is no doubt that Paul is saying we must confine our opinions about spiritual truth and morality to the teachings of the Bible, and be careful not to "go beyond what is written."

It is also possible that these words record for us a slogan that Paul and other Christians repeated regularly during the early days of the church. This section of text begins with the Greek article *to*, which is often used to introduce quoted material or a proverbial saying (cf. 1 Cor. 14:16). So the NIV translation may capture the essence of the verse best: "That you may learn from us the meaning of the saying, 'Do not go beyond what is written.' "

This would be a good slogan for Christians today to repeat regularly, similar to *sola scriptura,* the one made famous during the Reformation in Europe. It represents and reminds us of the important doctrine of the sufficiency of Scripture—both positively and negatively. Positively it reminds us that in God's Word we have all we need to know and serve Him—in other words, "everything pertaining to life and godliness" (2 Peter 1:3). And negatively the slogan reminds us that the Bible is the only trustworthy chart by which we can navigate the murky waters of human morality. As C. K. Barrett wrote, "The Corinthians were in danger of treating their own . . . traditions as if they were on the same level as Scripture."[5]

Whether the words of Paul in 1 Corinthians 4:6 are to be rendered as a warning or a command, we find in them a clear scriptural definition of what many have called "legalism." Legalism, in regard to Christian morality, is simply *creating moral standards beyond what the Scripture has revealed.* This can happen in the minds of individual Christians, causing them to be unnecessarily restricted in their own behavior and judgmental toward others who do not practice the same standard. And this problem can be evidenced and propagated by the teaching of Christian leaders and institutions, causing their adherents to labor under man-made rules and to impose those rules on others.

More Examples of Legalism

I have mentioned the examples of legalism that Paul encountered in Corinth, and in the other early churches, but it would be helpful at this point to consider some examples from the present day. And we can start with the Jack Hyles ad I mentioned at the beginning of the chapter. Was his mama a legalist, or not?

The answer, again with all due respect, is yes, she was being legalistic. I do not say that because she had rules in her household—that is the right and prerogative of any family, to determine what standards of behavior its members will abide by while they are in the home. But "Mama's teaching" went well beyond a biblical perspective, which would be, "These are the rules of our home, but we must be careful not to judge others in these areas." On the contrary, she taught her son "that such things as smoking, dancing, card-playing, movie-going and mixed bathing were *wrong*," clearly indicating that those activities are always displeasing to God.[6] But the Bible does not categorically condemn any of those activities, and so for her to categorically say they are wrong is legalism. And for her son's college to "follow Mama's teaching" instead of *scriptural* standards of morality is the epitome of legalism (see Mark 7:7–8). (And just in case you don't know, "mixed bathing" means males and females swimming together, not taking a bath together!)

Take smoking, for example, which is the activity on the Hyles list that the largest number of people would agree is wrong. It is fairly conventional wisdom among Christians (and even non-Christians these days!) that smoking is a sin. But where does this come from in the Bible? Do we really believe it is wrong for someone to enjoy a pipe once in a while, or smoke a cigar to celebrate a new baby? And as soon as we admit that periodic tobacco use is okay, we have called into question the validity of the statement that "smoking is a sin." "But," someone might say, "if you smoke cigarettes, or smoke a lot, that is a sin. Such smoking is harmful and addictive, and that makes it wrong, because the Bible says our body is the temple of the Holy Spirit (1 Cor. 6:19), and we should not be mastered by anything (v. 12)."

Think critically about that statement for a few moments with me. As you do, keep in mind that I never have smoked and never will, and my father died of lung cancer, so I have every reason in the world to dislike smoking and no reason to like it. I certainly do not recommend it as a wise thing to do, and I certainly realize that it is indeed wrong for many people to do it, if for no other reason than that their conscience is not clear about it (Rom. 14:23; see chapter 8). But does it follow, from the Bible passages alluded to in the preceding paragraph, that smoking is a sin in itself, or that God is always displeased with anyone who does it?

The first and most obvious fact is that the Bible does not mention smoking, which is understandable, because tobacco was apparently not available to people in Europe or the Middle East at the time the Bible was written.[7] But the Scriptures also do not mention any comparable substance with similar purposes and effects, like coffee, which did exist in the Middle East and is also potentially harmful and addictive. Alcohol, which is not entirely unlike tobacco in those ways, is mentioned in the Bible, but as we discussed in chapter 2, its use is allowed by God as long as it is used in moderation, with warnings about its addictive properties. No foods or dietary practices are treated as inherently sinful either, even though some of them may have been potentially harmful and addictive (yes, even in the pre-McDonalds world!). So although the Bible does not address the use of tobacco directly (that would be an anachronism), God could have easily spoken to similar practices—yet He did not.

But what about "your body is a temple of the Holy Spirit" (1 Cor. 6:19)? Doesn't that verse teach that we are not supposed to do anything that is harmful to our body? Well, if you believe that, then you definitely should not smoke, or do anything else that is harmful to your body in any way (like eating fast food). But I do not think you should say smoking is a sin for everybody, or judge anyone else, because the support from that verse is simply too thin and will not hold up under scrutiny. The context has nothing to do with health or dietary practices—Paul is saying that we should not commit sexual sin, because if we do we are becoming "one flesh" with a harlot; and since our bodies are a temple of the Holy Spirit, we would therefore be joining Him to the harlot (vv. 12–18). The main point is not that we are doing something bad to our body, but that we are doing something bad to the Holy Spirit when we sin against God, especially in that way.[8]

And what about "I will not be mastered by anything" (1 Cor. 6:12)? That verse speaks of a very important principle—that we must be careful not to let anything other than the Lord control us. But again, notice the context of the whole verse: "All things are lawful for me, but not all things are profitable. All things are lawful for me, but I will not be mastered by anything." If someone wants to apply this verse to an activity like smoking, then it actually would prove that smoking is not necessarily a sin in itself. Paul clearly says that he is talking about things that are "lawful" for him to do (not wrong in themselves), but then offers other considerations that help him to decide whether it is wise for him to do them. This and other passages of Scripture indicate that we can do things that are not wise, but still not be sinning against God. Or in other words, there is a difference between lacking wisdom and being disobedient.[9] I would also suggest that there is a difference between *sin* and *weakness*, and that for many people smoking falls into the latter category, much like eating too much or fingernail biting. These are not the *best* things to do for our health and reputation, but they do not necessarily alienate us from God.

One more thought for those who would still insist that "smoking is a sin": Would you say that someone has to stop smoking, or at least be willing to stop, in order to become a Christian, or to become a member of the church? Most Christians would make such a statement about someone who is involved in adultery. Yet is smoking not a different matter, precisely because it is not a clear scriptural issue? And what about current members of the church who smoke and do not stop? Should they be disciplined by the church and excommunicated because they are persisting in this "sin"? Again, I think such questions illustrate that there is a scriptural line drawn between activities like adultery and smoking, and that we should be careful not to blur that line.

Fools Rush In . . .

Finally, since I am "pushing the envelope" by talking about matters that are controversial among Christians (I'll explain why later on), let me go where angels fear to tread and address one that almost everyone will tend to disagree with me about. Recently I read a chapter in a book and an article in a magazine by two prominent and respected Christian leaders, explaining why all forms of gambling are sinful. Their arguments are so well-crafted and thoroughly laced with scriptural references that it is hard to imagine that anyone who respects them and the Word of God could end up disagreeing with their conclusions. But though they definitely prove that gambling is fraught with dangers for the Christian, and that for many people it is indeed a sin, I believe these teachers go too far by implying that it is always wrong, and therefore fall into a subtle form of legalism.[10]

First of all, the Bible simply does not mention gambling. None of the many verses quoted in the arguments against it are actually talking about gambling itself—inferences must be drawn from the passages to apply to the practice. And this is especially significant, because *gambling did exist* in the Greco-Roman world at the time the Bible was written. Furthermore, much of the case against gambling relates to the issue of motives. For instance, 1 Timothy 6:9 says, "Those who want to get rich fall into temptation and a snare and many foolish and harmful desires which plunge men into ruin and destruction." I believe that wanting to get rich is a sin, because the Bible says so, and therefore anyone who gambles with the goal and desire of getting rich is sinning. The sin is not the act of gambling, however, but the attitude of the heart. And it is simply not correct to assume that everyone who gambles does so out of a desire to get rich.

Imagine a man named Bill, who has gambled two times in his life, while on vacation in Atlantic City and Reno. In both cases he did it merely to have fun, and maybe to win enough to pay for his hotel room for that night. He took $20 with him to the casino, which is about what he might pay for other vacation fun, like video games or movies. He planned to leave when the $20 was gone, or when his set time limit was up, whichever came first. Both times he quit when his time limit was up, one time leaving with about the same amount of money he started with, and the second time with about $120. In the first case he was thanking God that he had a new experience that was enjoyable, and in the second case he was thanking God that his hotel room was paid for (see Romans 14:6 for why thanking God is important in situations like this).

Do I understand that gambling can be addictive and ruin someone's life? Yes. Do I understand that it is wrong to lust for money, or even to gamble with money that would otherwise be given to the Lord? Yes. Do I understand that gambling to earn money to pay bills or debts is an unscriptural approach to finances? Yes. Would I vote to keep gambling illegal in my state because of the bad effects it has on the culture? Yes. But do I think that it was necessarily wrong for Bill to enjoy those games for a couple hours on vacation? No, and I don't think I should judge others who might enjoy the "sport" of gambling even more often than twice in their lives.[11]

But, you might say, shouldn't we stay away from the possibility of sin? That kind of reasoning is what led Jack Hyles and his mama to say that card-playing of any kind is a sin (even when you are not betting on it). If you play with cards just for fun, you might end up gambling, and then you might end up addicted to it, and so on. The same goes for "mixed bathing"—if males and females of any age are allowed to swim together, it might lead to lust and sexual sin.

We will discuss more about the practice of constructing "fences" to keep people from sin, the favorite activity of the Pharisees, in chapter 7 of this book. But for now I am simply trying to help you to see that a categorical judgment about any practice not mentioned in Scripture, even one as potentially dangerous as gambling, is "going beyond what is written" and should be avoided. We can and should warn people about the dangers of such activities, and inform them about the scriptural issues that might relate to them, but we should stop short of saying that they are sinful in themselves. And we have to be very careful about "teaching as doctrines the precepts of men" (Mark 7:7), which is what happens when we elevate "Mama's teaching" (or anyone's teaching) to the level of Scripture.

At this point you may have some questions on your mind. One might be, "Is there anything that is a sin anymore?! I mean, if we can't say smoking and gambling are wrong, is holiness not an issue for a Christian?!" The answer is yes, holiness is *the most important issue* for a Christian, and there are thousands of impediments to it, discussed repeatedly in the Bible. But most of them are matters of the heart, and my concern is that when we focus on outward actions that the Bible does not even address, we are distracted from the attitudes in our heart, which are the real issues in our spirituality.[12] And that leads me to a second question that might be on your mind: "This seems like nit-picking or hair-splitting to me. Does it really matter whether godly Christian leaders, or any of us, cross the fine line that you are describing?" The answer to that question is also yes, because of the dangers that arise from even the most subtle forms of legalism—dangers which we will learn about in the next chapter.

Questions for Discussion and Application

1. What are some different ways you have heard the word "legalism" used? How do they compare to the definition given in this chapter?
2. What are some reasons why Paul would devote a whole chapter of 1 Corinthians to the subject of not "going beyond what is written"? Why is this issue so important to him?
3. Why do you think God gave us a written guidebook for the Christian life (the Bible), rather than speaking to us in a voice or vision, as he did with the people in ancient times? Are we better off than they, or worse?

4. This chapter uses smoking as an example to represent many other issues that are not mentioned in Scripture. Using it again as an example, how do you think calling smoking a sin could negatively affect people who do it? On the other hand, if they believed that they had freedom in this area, how might that help them? Which perspective do you think would make it easier for them to quit smoking?

CHAPTER FIVE

Two Dangers of Legalism

W hy is the apostle Paul so concerned, in 1 Corinthians 4, that Christians should never go
"beyond what is written" in their judgments about moral
issues? Why should we, as individuals and churches, be
so committed to guarding our hearts and words against
the error of legalism? The answer lies in all the problems
that result from it. One experienced pastor put it this way:

> If I were asked to name the major enemies of vital Chris-
> tianity today, I'm not sure but what I wouldn't name legal-
> ism first . . . it is a killer. It kills congregations when a pas-
> tor is a legalist. It kills pastors when congregations are
> legalistic. Legalistic people with their rigid do's and don'ts
> kill the spirit of joy and spontaneity of those who wish to
> enjoy their liberty. Strict legalistic people in leadership
> drain the very life out of a church, even though they may
> claim they are doing God a service.[1]

In the passage we have been considering, Paul discusses
two of the primary dangers of legalism—spiritual pride and
division in the body of Christ. First Corinthians 4:6 says,
"Now these things, brethren, I have figuratively applied to
myself and Apollos for your sakes, so that in us you may
learn not to exceed what is written, *so that no one of you*

will become arrogant in behalf of one against the other." The last part of that verse is a purpose clause (beginning with the Greek conjunction *hina*) explaining why Paul wants the Corinthians to keep themselves from going beyond what is written. And since his words are a part of the Word of God to every age, this passage tells all Christians in all eras why we should work so hard to keep ourselves from falling into even the most subtle forms of legalism.

The Danger of Spiritual Pride

Paul says we should avoid legalism "so that no one of you will become arrogant." First of all, notice that by saying "no one," he is implying that any Christian can fall into this error, and be threatened by this danger. Paul's use of this term at the beginning of the clause also weighs against a common interpretation that says he is referring to himself and Apollos when he refers to the "one" and "the other." On the contrary, the apostle is concerned that no one become arrogant—not just the factions arguing over the two ministers' qualifications.[2] You can become legalistic in any particular situation, no matter how spiritually mature you may be, or even how much you might hate legalism in others!

And when you are legalistic in a particular situation, or concerning a particular issue, it will cause in you *spiritual pride*, which has serious ramifications for your relationship with God and others (see Prov. 16:18; Matt. 23:12; James 4:6; 1 Peter 5:5, etc.). Paul clearly says that this is the case, but how exactly does it happen? We can learn more about this danger by looking at the Greek word Paul uses (*physiaō*, translated "become arrogant"). The word literally means "to be puffed up," and is found several other times in Paul's writings.

1 Corinthians 8:1–3. In this passage the apostle says, "Now concerning things sacrificed to idols, we know that we all have knowledge. Knowledge makes arrogant [*physiaō*], but love edifies. If anyone supposes that he knows anything, he has not yet known as he ought to know; but if anyone loves God, he is known by Him."

We will learn more about the issue of "things sacrificed to idols" in chapter 8 of this book, but for now notice Paul's concern that "knowledge makes arrogant," or as the KJV reads, "knowledge puffeth up." The study of spiritual issues can actually produce bad results if it is divorced from the love for God and others that should be the purpose of all learning. As 1 Timothy 1:5 says, "The goal of our instruction is love from a pure heart and a good conscience and a sincere faith." When love is not the goal of our learning, it is never the result. Instead, the knowledge we gain just makes us prideful and unloving toward others. Along these lines, it is interesting to notice how many judgmental and legalistic conversations begin with words like "I've studied this extensively," "I've been around the block a few times," or "*I know* why this is happening." The more people think they know about a particular issue, through study or experience, the more qualified they feel to make judgments about it—even if the Scriptures do not make such judgments.

Colossians 2:18. Paul uses the same word in this verse when he describes the kind of person who is "inflated [*physiaō*] without cause by his fleshly mind." Read the whole context of that verse, and you will see that it directly relates to our topic, and sheds more light on it:

> Therefore no one is to act as your judge in regard to food or drink or in respect to a festival or a new moon or a Sab-

bath day—things which are a mere shadow of what is to come; but the substance belongs to Christ. Let no one keep defrauding you of your prize by delighting in self-abasement and the worship of the angels, taking his stand on visions he has seen, inflated without cause by his fleshly mind, and not holding fast to the head, from whom the entire body, being supplied and held together by the joints and ligaments, grows with a growth which is from God.

If you have died with Christ to the elementary principles of the world, why, as if you were living in the world, do you submit yourself to decrees, such as, "Do not handle, do not taste, do not touch!" (which all refer to things destined to perish with use)—in accordance with the commandments and teachings of men? These are matters which have, to be sure, the appearance of wisdom in self-made religion and self-abasement and severe treatment of the body, but are of no value against fleshly indulgence. (Col. 2:16–23)

Notice that all the problems Paul addresses in that passage are forms of "going beyond what is written." Some Jewish Christians were saying that the Gentile Christians were required to continue obeying Old Testament rituals that had been fulfilled in Christ (vv. 16–17). Others were promoting asceticism (self-denial not mandated by Scripture) and mysticism (additional revelation not found in Scripture) as ways of growing closer to God (v. 18). And still others were deriving a list of "Christian taboos" from "the commandments and teachings of men" rather than from God's Word (vv. 20–22). I can't imagine a passage more relevant to our topic, and to the problems in the church today—even though it was written almost two thousand years ago!

But notice also how Paul alludes to the bad results of "going beyond what is written." The first one he mentions is spiritual pride—some of the Colossians were "inflated," or puffed up, by their extrabiblical visions (v. 18). And when he addresses people who add extra rules to the Scriptures, he says that although they may appear very spiritual, they really are not. Their man-made traditions are "of no value against fleshly indulgence" (v. 23). This is such an important truth to understand about legalism: it offers one thing, but delivers the opposite. Instead of making us more spiritually mature and godly, it actually renders us immature and ungodly in various ways. The more we add to the Scriptures, the more we go backward instead of forward in our relationship with God.

The Bible clearly states this in Colossians 2:23, so we know it is a truth from the Word of God. But I have also seen this axiom proven true time and time again in my own experience. To mention just one example that I encountered recently: My wife and I were once in a home-school support group with a couple who were very legalistic in their approach to the Christian life. They would never think of listening to any music with drums in it, would never touch alcohol, and had nine children because they thought birth control was a sin. Not long ago, I heard that although the man was respected at church for his high standards and extensive service, he had a terrible reputation among his colleagues at work. Then recently I found out that he had become convinced by a "revelation from God" that his wife was going to die soon, so he sought a replacement for her by having an affair with her best friend. This couple's life was filled with extrabiblical asceticism and mysticism, but that did not bring them closer to God. In fact, they found themselves far away from Him. That may be an extreme example, but remember that to whatever extent you go beyond what is written, it will short-circuit your spiritual growth to the same degree.

Why does this happen? One way of explaining it is that when we are learning and obeying the commandments and teachings of Scripture, the Holy Spirit is present and working within us as we do (see the parallel passages in Eph. 5:18–19 and Col. 3:16). But when we are learning and obeying the "commandments and teachings of men," He is not. If we grow in our godliness by the power of the Holy Spirit, He makes sure that we progress in humility as well. But when we are living in legalism by our own strength, we can only grow arrogant as we surpass other Christians in our "spiritual success."

There are many other ways that legalism works against true godliness, which we will discuss further in chapter 7. But by addressing spiritual pride first in 1 Corinthians 4:6, Paul is putting his finger on the primary inward problem that leads to so many others, and in his next words he exposes the outward result that bothers him the most.

Division in the Body of Christ

Paul says, ". . . that no one of you will become arrogant *in behalf of one against the other.*" Legalism inevitably leads to spiritual pride, and spiritual pride inevitably leads to division among believers. Differing standards of morality, and the judgments based on them, pit brother against brother, and groups of Christians against other groups of Christians. An "us against them" mentality almost always develops when we go beyond what is written.

A few examples should help you to see how this progression takes place. Suppose a couple have become convinced by some teaching they have heard that God's way of feeding a baby is "parent-controlled" rather than "demand feeding." Of course the Bible does not say anything directly about when we should feed our infants, but arguments against "demand feeding" have been inferred from the fact that God is a God of order not chaos, and the principle that a family should not be child-centered. So this couple have become convinced that scheduled feeding is morally superior to feeding babies whenever they seem to be hungry.

Now suppose they meet another couple in their church who do not follow the "parent-controlled" plan. Perhaps this other couple not only feed their child "on demand," but also practice other taboos like sharing a bed with their little one, rocking her to sleep at night, or even driving her around the block in the car seat to get her calmed down. What are the first couple going to think of this second couple who are so "child-centered"? Would they be likely to become friends with them, or share a Bible study or family worship with them? No, the only relationship they will develop with them will probably be an attempt to "help" them, or straighten them out on their bad parenting practices. Then if the child-centered couple don't change, they will be seen in an even worse light, because they do not take counsel very well! Before long, this church may end up with two separate factions, the enlightened "parent-controlled feeding" group versus everyone else who does not realize how important this issue is for the health and future of our families!

Another example is the belief and teaching that churches must practice weekly communion. Observing the Lord's Supper every Sunday is certainly acceptable to Christ, who said, "As often as you eat this bread and drink the cup, you proclaim the Lord's death until He comes" (1 Cor. 11:26). There is no scriptural reason why a church cannot do this on a weekly basis. But there is also no sound exegetical evidence that the Lord's Supper *must* be observed every time we gather for worship. It seems that the Lord has given us freedom regarding the frequency of the observance—implied in the words "as often as you eat."[3]

But suppose the leaders in a particular church teach that the Lord's Supper is such a necessary part of worship that we have not really worshipped without it. They say the service "should never end without Communion. . . . On the Lord's Day God invites us to His house for a meal. . . . The Lord's Supper ought to be a normal part of our weekly worship. Period."[4] So what will the members of that church tend to think about another body that does not practice weekly communion? What if they visit a church while traveling, and there is no communion on that particular Sunday? Will they think that they have not really worshipped the Lord, and say that about the brothers and sisters there ("At our church, we *really* worship")? What if they move to another area where there is no church that practices weekly communion—will they break apart from a good one to form their own "weekly communion" church? Add a few other issues into the mix, like "paedocommunion" and "the necessity of Christian education," and you have what has actually happened in many communities.[5] There is division caused among believers because of a preoccupation with issues that are not clearly addressed in the Scriptures.

I understand that some division between Christians is a "necessary evil," especially at the local church level, because the doctrinal differences are significant enough for the people involved. I myself once left a Baptist church to start a Presbyterian church because a group of us believed that we needed to teach and practice what we were learning from the Word of God. So I do not mean to cast suspicion on all believers who are unable to remain in an existing church. But I do want to challenge all of us to consider the kinds of issues that would cause us to criticize other Christians, or the leadership in a particular church. Are these issues really biblical ones, or are they mere preferences, or extrapolations from biblical principles that do not hold up under careful scrutiny?

Division between believers in Christ is sometimes necessary for clearly biblical reasons, but division for any other reason, especially if it involves sinful judging, is abhorrent to God. Notice what Solomon says in Proverbs 6:16–19: "There are six things which the LORD hates, yes, seven which are an abomination to Him: Haughty eyes, a lying tongue, and hands that shed innocent blood, a heart that devises wicked plans, feet that run rapidly to evil, a false witness who utters lies, and *one who spreads strife among brothers.*" In that passage, Solomon is probably employing a literary device that is used elsewhere in Proverbs (cf. 30:18–19) to emphasize how bad the last item on the list is. He associates division among brothers— something that might be considered unavoidable and not very serious—with a group of other sins that are already known to be repugnant to God. So he wants us to know that division in the family of God is something that should be avoided at all costs (except at the cost of biblical truth, of course). And he especially warns us not to be the one who causes such unnecessary division by, for instance, spreading legalistic ideas that will drive a wedge between Christians.

The oft-quoted maxim, though it has been misused at times, is still a good one to consider:

> In essentials, unity;
> In non-essentials, liberty;
> In all things, charity.

"Charity" means love, of course, and that brings us back to 1 Corinthians 8:1—"Knowledge makes arrogant, but love edifies." Beware of the tendency to become proud of the things you learn from the Scriptures—let alone the things that are not from the Bible! Don't let your convictions create an unnecessary wall between you and other believers. And even if you must disagree on matters that are discussed in the Word of God, bathe that disagreement in humility and kindness, treating the other person as you would want to be treated.

Smoking and Gambling Again

In chapter 4 I split some hairs in saying that smoking and gambling are wrong for many people because of the motivations and mastery involved, but we should not say that those practices are always sinful or wrong in themselves. In this chapter I have tried to explain why it is worth splitting hairs on issues like this. The dangers of legalism are too great for us to tolerate it in even the most subtle form. So for the conclusion of this chapter, let me use those two examples again, to summarize and remind you of what we have learned.

If you believe that smoking and gambling (and other similar practices) are sinful in themselves, you will run the risk of developing a proud attitude toward people who engage in them. You will think yourself more spiritual than they, at least in this area, and tend to treat them differently because of it. If it was a clear scriptural issue, like adultery or heresy, you would still have to fight the tendency to think yourself better, but the Holy Spirit would be working through the Word, helping you to address the situation with love and humility. But when you go beyond what is written, no such empowerment is provided. It is just your preference against theirs, and you are more likely to fall into the trap of spiritual pride.

If you go further than the Scriptures go in regard to activities like smoking and gambling, you may also cause unnecessary division among Christians. It will be difficult for you to have unhindered fellowship with people who practice such things, because you will hesitate to befriend them, and vice versa. In the context of a church family, this can create significant problems for ministry. I have been in churches where smoking and gambling were labeled as sins. Guess how many people who smoked or gambled attended those churches: only a few who were willing to lead a double life and hide those practices from everyone else. Most people who smoked or gambled just avoided those churches like the plague! This meant that many Christians who were actually growing in Christ could not feel at home in the church and be blessed by the body there. And it also meant that many unbelievers were unnecessarily turned away from a place where they could get to know God.

Wouldn't it be much better for church leaders and members to say something like "The Bible doesn't say these things are wrong in themselves," and then talk about the related issues of the heart, which are more important anyway? This would allow people the freedom to examine the issues for themselves, and in regard to their own hearts, which would lead them closer to true spirituality. And it would keep others from looking down on them, or holding them at arm's length.

So legalism leads to spiritual pride, which in turn leads to division in the body of Christ. And one of the biggest answers to both of those problems, according to Paul, is to "learn not to exceed what is written." But Paul goes on in the next verse to point out an interesting irony. Not only is the problem of pride a result of legalism, but pride is also often a cause of the problem of legalism. So in the next chapter we will learn how to develop true humility, which is the greatest antidote to the disease of legalism, whether we are trying to prevent its onset, or to cure it after we have already been infected.

Questions for Discussion and Application

1. First Corinthians 8:1 says "knowledge puffeth up" (KJV). How does that happen?
2. Read Colossians 2:16–23 again. In what ways were the Colossians going beyond what is written, and how do people today do similar things?
3. Now that you have learned about legalism and read many examples of it, do you think you have been legalistic in any way in the past? Are you now?
4. Think about other Christians you know that you are not very close friends with, or perhaps not friends at all. Have any extrabiblical beliefs or preferences contributed to the distance between you and them?

CHAPTER SIX

Pride Questioned and Convicted

A ccording to the Scriptures, the sin of pride is positively criminal. It will rob you of the blessing of God in your life and wreak violence on your relationships with other people. Consider these verses from the book of Proverbs:

When pride comes, then comes dishonor, but with the humble is wisdom. (11:2)

Everyone who is proud in heart is an abomination to the LORD; assuredly, he will not be unpunished. (16:5)

Pride goes before destruction, and a haughty spirit before stumbling. It is better to be humble in spirit with the lowly than to divide the spoil with the proud. (16:18–19)

Do you see a man wise in his own eyes? There is more hope for a fool than for him. (26:12)

An arrogant man stirs up strife, but he who trusts in the LORD will prosper. (28:25)

A man's pride will bring him low, but a humble spirit will obtain honor. (29:23)

Three times in the Gospels, Jesus says, "Whoever exalts himself shall be humbled; and whoever humbles himself shall be exalted" (Matt. 23:12; cf. Luke 14:11; 18:14). James and Peter both say that "God is opposed to the proud, but gives grace to the humble" (James 4:6; 1 Peter 5:5). And in the text we have been discussing in this book, the apostle Paul singles out the sin of pride and subjects it to the biblical equivalent of a brutal interrogation.

The sin of pride is so connected to judging and legalism that it is not only a result, but also a source of those problems. In 1 Corinthians 4:6, the apostle Paul says that going beyond what is written leads to arrogance, and in the next verse he implies that the converse is also true. In 1 Corinthians 4:7 he "catechizes" his readers with three questions that will convict us of the pride that our judging and legalism have produced, but will also help us to avoid them in the first place. In chapter 3 of this book I suggested five questions we should ask to cross-examine our judgments; here Paul is suggesting three questions that can counteract any kind of legalistic thinking: "For who regards you as superior? What do you have that you did not receive? And if you did receive it, why do you boast as if you had not received it?"

Searching questions like these must be asked and understood if the guilt of our pride is to be exposed. Like a criminal, our pride needs to be convicted, but also like a criminal (especially one with a good lawyer), it can be rather slippery and difficult to bring to justice. As Charles Spurgeon said, "If killed, pride revives. If buried, it bursts the tomb. You may hunt down this fox and think you have destroyed it, and lo, your very exultation is pride."[1] The great English preacher also added that even when praying for humility, we may still be proud: "Men proudly ask to be humble. They desire to be humble in order that they may be admired for it."[2]

The difficulty of killing pride is illustrated by a story I heard once about the famous American preacher Harry Ironside. When Harry was a young man, he realized that he had a problem with pride. So he went to the elders of his church and asked them what he should do about it. They suggested that he make a big sign saying "Repent or Perish," or something like that, and walk up and down the busiest street in Chicago all day long, holding the sign. So Harry did what they suggested, and after enduring a whole day of jeers and mockery from the crowds, he thought to himself, "Hmmm, not everybody would have done that!"

Even if you are not struggling with judging and legalism at this time, I am sure that you have to fight against pride, because we all do. And if you do not win that fight, you will likely become the kind of person who goes beyond what is written, because you will think too highly of your own opinions, and place them on a par with the Scriptures. When you have already fallen into the errors of judging and legalism, on the other hand, confronting your pride and developing a true humility will be one of the main solutions to those problems. So because of the subtle deceits of pride, and because of its destructive effects, we desperately need to understand the questions that Paul asks in 1 Corinthians 4:7, and constantly ask them of ourselves.

Question #1: "Who regards you as superior?"

In this first question, Paul uses the Greek verb *krinō* again ("to judge"), but adds a prefix to make it *diakrinō*, which means "to judge between" or "to make a difference between" two people. The King James Version renders the question quite literally, "Who maketh thee to differ?" But the newer versions, and some amplified ones, capture the meaning very well:

NASB: "Who regards you as superior?"
ESV: "For who sees anything different in you?"
NIV: "Who makes you different from anyone else?"
Moffatt: "Who singles you out?"

Perhaps the tone of Paul's question is best communicated by "Who in the world sees anything special in you?" He is "slamming" the Corinthians, putting them in their place. He is speaking in a colloquial manner, or in other words, using first-century slang to express his disgust at their stupidity. If he were writing in the modern world, he might say something like, "You think you're so great? NOT!" Or he might have used words like "Hello!" or "Get a clue!"

This question reminds me of a passion play that I will never forget—not because it was so well produced and acted, but because of a lady sitting behind me in the audience who made loud comments during various parts of the performance. During the woman-caught-in-adultery scene, for instance, after Jesus had said that he who is without sin should cast the first stone, the accusers on the stage started dropping the rocks they were holding, one by one. Finally, the ringleader was the only one with a rock left in his hand, and in a dramatic moment he hesitated, looking at the rock, then at Jesus, then at the adulteress, then back at the rock again. At this point, the woman in the audience yelled out, "Put it down!" And sure enough, he did.

A little later in the play the actor playing Satan pranced back and forth across the stage, gloating in his "victory" over Christ at the crucifixion. "Who is the Lord now?" he snarled rhetorically, and the woman answered him from her seat: "Not you, honey!" Finally, when the same character turned his taunts to God Himself, boasting of how powerful he was, the unbilled star behind me shouted, "Who do you think you are?!"

Those stories contain good examples of pride—the people who thought they were better than the adulterous woman, Satan thinking he was more powerful than God—but my point in telling them is to illustrate the tone of Paul's question to the Corinthians. In fact, "Who do you think you are?!" is fairly close to the question itself.

So Paul's first question is primarily designed to get his readers' attention and rebuke them with its tone, but it is also helpful to consider it in more depth. Think about it for a moment: Who *does* regard you as superior? The answer is . . . *only you.* You are the only one who considers yourself to be superior to others—nobody else does! Go ahead and ask others if they think you are a superior person, and see what they say. Or better yet, ask them to list the weaknesses they have seen in you, and you will no longer be under any illusion about your superior character. Your delusions of grandeur will quickly fade under their more objective evaluation.

Here is another "Shoes Principle" to go along with the one I mentioned in chapter 3 (putting yourself in others' shoes, to see how you should treat them). This one has a different twist, and comes from that eminent theologian, Bob Dylan. In his song "Positively 4th Street," Dylan sings,

> I wish that for just one time
> You could stand inside my shoes,
> And just for that one moment
> I could be you.

> Yes, I wish that for just one time
> You could stand in my shoes;
> You'd know what a drag it is
> To see you.[3]

Though it may come from a surprising source, there is some profound biblical wisdom in those lyrics. If you really want to get an accurate picture of yourself, learn to look at yourself through the eyes of others. Their perspective will be much closer to the truth, because it is our nature to think more highly of ourselves than we ought (Rom. 12:3). We tend to see the best in us and the worst in others. As someone once said (I don't think this was Bob Dylan), "Pride hides a man's faults to himself, and magnifies them to everyone else." So if you do not want to be ensnared by the deceptive powers of pride, ask yourself this question: "Who regards you as superior?"

But you might protest, "What if I *am* better than someone else in some way? That is possible, isn't it?" Yes it is, and that is why Paul asks his second question . . .

Question #2: "What do you have that you did not receive?"

As one commentator says, "The first question deals with an imaginary possession, the second with an actual possession which one may misuse for puffing himself up."[4] Paul knew that the Corinthians, and all the other readers of his letter, might answer his first question with a list of character qualities and good deeds that separate them from others. So with his next question, he summarily addresses everything that we might claim to have that is good in our lives. And as another commentator writes, "This question is an invitation to experience one of those rare, unguarded moments of total honesty, where in the presence of the eternal God one recognizes that everything, absolutely *everything*, that one has is a gift."[5]

Think about anything that is good in your life. You did not produce it, you did not earn it, and you do not have the power in yourself to keep it. As James 1:17 says, "Every good thing given and every perfect gift is from above, coming down from the Father of lights." "Every good thing" means every good thing, obviously, but because we tend to be so thick and forgetful about this, it would be helpful to consider some examples of the good things we have received from God.

First, consider *good things that you did not work for*, like natural intelligence and talents, education that was provided for you when you were younger, good health, and wealth inherited from your parents. Inasmuch as you contributed nothing whatsoever to receiving these gifts, how can you look down on others who do not have them? Charles Spurgeon's words about one particular gift are typically pointed and profound:

> The same is true of beauty of person, which too frequently is the cause of vanity. Beauty is often a snare on this account. What if thy features be delicately chiselled, what if thine eyes are bright as the morning, and thy countenance fair as the lily, what if there be a charm in thine every glance; what hast thou in all these for which to praise thyself? Jezebel also was fair to look upon, and is she to be praised? Is not thy beauty the gift of God? Bless thy Creator for it, but do not despise those who are less comely, for in so doing thou wilt despise their Maker. How often do we hear a laugh raised behind their backs against persons who are somewhat grotesque, or may be deformed, but God made them, and who is he that shall dare to taunt

the Maker with what he has done? What hast thou, O thou fairest among women; what hast thou, O thou comeliest among the sons of men, but what thou hast received? Cease, then, those mincing airs and tossings of the head.[6]

Now consider *good things that you think you have earned*, like success in higher education, business, sports, love, family, etc. Who gave you the ability to achieve that success? Who kept your heart beating and your lungs breathing while you did that? Man is an *utterly dependent creature*. We do not cause ourselves to be born or keep ourselves living, let alone exercise control over the outcome of our efforts. And man is also a *corrupt creature*, deserving nothing good from a holy God, but only judgment in hell for the many sins we have all committed (Gen. 6:5; Matt. 5:21–30; Rom. 3:23; 6:23). "But I'm a Christian," you might say, "I'm forgiven, because I've repented from my sins and have faith in Christ." That is correct—you are forgiven if you have repentance and faith, but even your repentance and faith are gifts of God, from whom you have *received* them! Consider the following verses:

> And [Jesus] was saying, "For this reason I have said to you, that no one can come to Me, unless it has been granted him from the Father." (John 6:65)

> He is the one whom God exalted to His right hand as a Prince and a Savior, to grant repentance to Israel, and forgiveness of sins. (Acts 5:31)

> When they heard this, they quieted down and glorified God, saying, "Well then, God has granted to the Gentiles also the repentance that leads to life." (Acts 11:18)

With gentleness correcting those who are in opposition, if perhaps God may grant them repentance leading to the knowledge of the truth. (2 Tim. 2:25)

For to you it has been granted for Christ's sake, not only to believe in Him, but also to suffer for His sake. (Phil. 1:29)

For by grace you have been saved through faith; and that not of yourselves, it is the gift of God; not as a result of works, so that no one may boast. (Eph. 2:8–9)

So being a Christian definitely separates you from people who are not, but it does not make you superior to them. You have merely *received* God's gracious provision, because Jesus Christ earned righteousness for you by living a perfect life and dying a substitutionary death on the cross. "For the wages of sin [what you have earned] is death, but the free gift of God [what you could never earn] is eternal life in Christ Jesus our Lord" (Rom. 6:23).

Nor should you become proud of your spiritual advancement beyond other Christians, though you may indeed be farther along than some of them. Again, Spurgeon lets us have it right between the eyes:

Perhaps, my dear brother, there is a difference between you and other saints. I am sure there is reason for some saints to eclipse others, for some professors are very poor things indeed. Well, brother, you have a great deal more faith than others; where did you get it? If you received it from anywhere but from God, you had better get rid of it. Dear brother, you have more joy than some, and possibly you feel ashamed of your fellow Christians who are so doubting and sad: beware that you do not become vain of your joy, and remember, that if your joy is true joy you received it of the Lord. Are you more useful than others? You cannot help looking at certain professors who are idle, and wishing that you could stir them up. I know I do; I would put a sharp pin into their downy cushions if I could: but for all that, who gives us activity, who gives us usefulness, who gives us zeal, who gives us courage, who gives us everything? If you, dear friend, get into such a condition that you begin to whisper to yourself, "I have improved my gifts and graces at a very noble rate, and am getting on exceedingly well in spiritual things," you will soon have to come down from your high places. . . . Blessed is the man who lies low at the foot of the cross, and who, concerning everything that he has, whether temporal or spiritual, ascribes all to the Giver of all Good.[7]

What this means practically is that when you start to think thoughts like "I deserve better than this" or "I don't deserve to be treated like that," you need to take those thoughts captive to the obedience of Christ (2 Cor. 10:5). Change them to thoughts like "O Lord, You deserve all glory" or "You deserve my thanks for the good things that I do have." This will keep you from falling under the judgment King Herod received in Acts 12:21–23: "On an appointed day Herod, having put on his royal apparel, took his seat on the rostrum and began delivering an address to them. The people kept crying out, 'The voice of a god and not of a man!' And immediately an angel of the Lord struck him because he did not give God the glory, and he was eaten by worms and died."

Notice that Herod did not even boast or praise himself during that incident—he simply failed to thank God, and give Him the glory. Obviously he was ignoring the truth that anything good we have comes from God, and in a powerful example for all of us, he lost his life because of it. In

Isaiah 42:8 God says, "I am the LORD, that is My name; I will not give My glory to another." So if we do not give Him the glory for good things we have, sooner or later they will inevitably be taken from us.

On the other hand, when we realize that everything good we have is a gift from God, and live in light of that truth, we will be thankful people who will be much less likely to fall into the errors of judgmentalism and legalism. John Fischer explains this well in his book *12 Steps for a Recovering Pharisee*:

> There isn't one pharisaical characteristic Jesus spoke out against that is not stripped of its power by a thankful heart. No need to judge other people when you are thankful for who you are. No need to measure yourself by and compare yourself to others when you are thankful for what God has done in your life. No need to stand at the door of the kingdom of God and keep others out when you're just thankful that you got in. God can let in anyone he wants. It's up to him. You are simply glad to be counted among the saved.
>
> You don't care if you get the important seat at the table when you are overcome with gratitude at simply being invited to the dinner. You don't put heavy weights on other people's shoulders when you are thankful that God has lightened your own load. You are not obsessed with what other people think of you when you are overwhelmed with the fact that God is thinking about you all the time. You don't demand respect when you are thankful for your place. You don't have to hide your own sin when you have received God's forgiveness. You don't have to maintain an outward show when God has cleaned up your heart. You don't have to protect your image when you are already number one with God. You don't have to condemn other people's blindness when it's only the grace of God that has

allowed you to see. You don't have to try for the highest place when you are already grateful for the lowest. You don't have to make a show of spirituality when you are thankful for having received the Spirit. You don't have to clothe yourself in holy robes when you already have been clothed in righteousness. You don't have to be full of yourself when you are thankful that God has filled you up with himself.[8]

Question #3: "And if you did receive it, why do you boast as if you had not received it?"

A better translation of the first part of this question would be "*since* you did receive it" (Greek: *ei de kai*). Paul makes clear that everything good we have has been received as a gift from God. But then his interrogation of pride builds to a climax with his third question, which is designed to show the utter sinfulness of this sin. It is not enough for us to imagine in our minds that we are superior to other people, and take credit in our own hearts for things we did not earn—we add insult to injury by expressing those foolish thoughts with our mouths! We brag to others as if we ourselves had produced the good things we have.

Proverbs 27:2 says, "Let another praise you, and not your own mouth; a stranger, and not your own lips." And Proverbs 30:32 adds, "If you have been foolish in exalting yourself . . . put your hand on your mouth." The wise man says we should stop ourselves before we begin praising or exalting ourselves. But to do this, we need to realize that there are different forms of boasting or bragging.

One form of this sin is obvious: "Hey, look at me, I'm great!" This type of boasting may have found its ultimate expression in a country song by Mac Davis:

Oh Lord, it's hard to be humble
When you're perfect in every way;
I can't wait to look in the mirror
'Cause I get better looking each day.

To know me is to love me,
I must be one @#%! of a man;
Oh Lord, it's hard to be humble,
But I'm doing the best that I can.

Everyone knows that is boasting, but most occurrences of the sin are not so blatant. There are a number of more subtle ways in which we can dishonor the Lord by boasting. According to 1 Corinthians 4:7, we should speak in a way that indicates no difference between ourselves and others, and recognizes that everything we have is a gift from God. So if we speak in any other way, we are committing the sin that God is talking about in this verse.

An example of this more subtle form of boasting is saying good things about yourself when it is not necessary—introducing your abilities or accomplishments into a conversation when it has no other purpose than to make you look good. Another example would be talking about yourself more than you talk about others. Truly humble people experience a "holy hesitation" when they talk about themselves, and they will do so only when the intention is to edify, encourage, or evangelize others. And finally, we are boasting when we put others down to build ourselves up. So much of our criticism of others, especially when it is spoken *about* them rather than *to* them, has the goal of making us look superior in the eyes of the listeners. But though we think that our words are tipping the scales of esteem in our favor, the result is that people end up resenting our critical spirit, or at the very least, they will be less likely to trust us when they hear us putting others down. So with every bad word we speak about others, the scales are really tipping away from us. Eventually we will be "weighed on the scales and found deficient," as God said to the proud and boastful king of Babylon in Daniel 5:27.

In Matthew 6:1–5 Jesus speaks of another form of sinful boasting, which was practiced by the legalists of His day:

> Beware of practicing your righteousness before men to be noticed by them; otherwise you have no reward with your Father who is in heaven. So when you give to the poor, do not sound a trumpet before you, as the hypocrites do in the synagogues and in the streets, so that they may be honored by men. Truly I say to you, they have their reward in full. . . . When you pray, you are not to be like the hypocrites; for they love to stand and pray in the synagogues and on the street corners so that they may be seen by men. Truly I say to you, they have their reward in full.

Two times in that passage, and again in Matthew 6:16, Jesus says that the hypocrites "have their reward in full" because they made sure that others knew about their good deeds. This has given rise to a custom in our household, that whenever someone brags about something good he or she has done, we say, "Oops! You just lost your reward!" We have found that this is a good reminder to "let another praise you, and not your own mouth." Our goal and prayer should be the same as the apostle Paul's in Galatians 6:14: "May it never be that I would boast, except in the cross of our Lord Jesus Christ, through which the world has been crucified to me, and I to the world."

Pride and Legalism

By now you should know the answers to Paul's catechism in 1 Corinthians 4:7: Who regards you as superior? (*Nobody*, except you!) "What do you have that you did not receive?" (*Nothing.*) And "Why do you boast as if you had not received it?" (*Nonsense*, utter nonsense!)

Hopefully you can see how these questions, and their answers, apply to the topic of this book. Pride is both a source and a result of the errors of judging and legalism. But Paul also may have had another connection in mind. Since everything good comes from God, anything that does not come from God is not good, particularly in our opinions about others. If the judgments you make about others are not from God—not based on His Word and guided by His Holy Spirit—then they are bad judgments and will have bad results. If the moral standards you promote have not been received from God, but have merely been invented by you or some other human being, those moral standards will not promote true godliness.

The fact is, judging and legalism are contrary to faith—they are ways of acting as if we are independent of God. We are acting as if we don't need Him to tell us how to view our brother or sister, and we don't need His Word to define sin and holiness, in our lives and in others' lives. When we go beyond what is written, we are basically saying to God, "I can decide on my own what is right and wrong and true and false. I don't need You to tell me." But on the other hand, the humble heart says, "I am not capable of discerning truth by my own abilities. I must stick as closely to the Word as possible, and not go beyond it, or I will surely go astray."

Questions for Discussion and Application

1. The early church father Augustine once said that the three most important qualities for a Christian to have are "first, humility; second, humility; and third, humility." Why do you think this character trait is so important?

2. Have you had any experiences where another person was used by God to humble you, perhaps in a sudden and dramatic fashion (à la "Who do you think you are?!")? Are you glad for that experience?

3. What are five things about your life that you are grateful for? Think about how you are dependent upon God for each of them, and why you should thank Him for each of them.

4. Why do legalistic people often seem to give off an aura of pridefulness, and why are people who seem prideful so often legalistic?

CHAPTER SEVEN

Jesus and Legalism

W hen I first read the Gospels in their entirety as a young Christian, I was in a legalistic environment, and I was amazed at how often Jesus encountered and interacted with this problem. In fact, confronting and correcting legalism seemed to be one of the primary themes of our Lord's earthly ministry. For many years I wondered if perhaps I was over-reacting to my situation at the time and reading this emphasis into the Scriptures. But recently I have spent two years preaching through the book of Luke in a very different environment, and this issue of legalism stills leaps off the page over and over again.

I am convinced that the reason this problem is so prevalent in the New Testament is that God knew that all Christians in all times would face it in one form or another. So in His sovereign plan, He allowed legalism to form much of the content of the controversies that both Jesus and the apostles faced in the first century, so that we could learn from them how to face it in our day. We have already discussed much of what the apostle Paul had to say about legalism in the earlier chapters of this book, but in this chapter we will learn about what Jesus thought about it.

The particular form of legalism that dominated Jewish life in the days of Christ was what He called "the leaven of the Pharisees." The Pharisees were a sect of Jewish religious leaders known for their zeal for God and devotion to His law. They were highly respected members of their society, considered by most to be the Jewish equivalent of what we would call "really committed Christians." But their commitment went beyond God and His law, as Robert Coleman explains:

> [The Pharisees] had so much respect for the original set of scriptures and wanted to protect them so desperately that they started adding to them. Then, after a while, it not only seemed helpful to make additions but absolutely essential. . . .
>
> The Pharisees were desperately determined to not break the laws of God. Consequently they devised a system to keep them from even coming close to angering God. They contrived a "fence" of Pharisaic rules that, if man would keep them, would guarantee a safe distance between himself and the laws of God. Therefore, if God said we could not work on the Sabbath, then don't even pick grain to eat, just to play it safe. Don't even heal people because that might be a borderline case. . . .
>
> The "fence" or "hedge" laws accumulated into hundreds over the years and were passed around orally. Soon it became apparent that they were far from optional. These laws became every inch as important as the scriptural laws and in some instances more crucial. . . .
>
> [The Pharisees] also saw their mission as creating new laws as the times changed. If they felt the Scriptures contained no moral laws to control something modern, then they would manufacture a law and announce that it was henceforth binding on man and God. New situations could not be ignored, and if there were gaps in the Scriptures, someone had to fill them. . . .

Jesus found it very difficult to appreciate a human being's changing God's laws. For him, it was fine if the Pharisees wanted to fast twice a week. They could go to it with great pleasure. The flak came when they said, "We instituted this new law, and God expects you to keep it." At this point Jesus balked and invited them to back off.[1]

As I mentioned before, this controversy between Jesus and the Pharisees is intensely practical for our lives two thousand years later:

It is just as easy for the modern believer to become blind to the gangrene that has spread through the church which is sometimes filled with teachings and traditions of purely human origin but that have over the years become so ingrained that they now appear to be of divine origin. Not that there is anything wrong with traditional practices or even with a church's local distinction. However, there is something desperately wrong with presenting these personal preferences as Divine truth.[2]

So taking a closer look at our Lord's interaction with the Pharisees will help us to understand how to keep sinful judging and legalism at bay in our own lives. He confronted their tendency to go "beyond what is written" many times, but the longest passage about this issue in the Gospels is found in Mark 7:1–23. In that passage, which we will use as a framework for this chapter, Jesus warns us about three more bad results of legalism. The apostle Paul taught about spiritual pride and division among Christians in 1 Corinthians 4, but here Jesus adds *hypocrisy, neglect of the Word, and false spirituality.*

Hypocrisy

Mark 7:1–4 tells us about the "traditions of the elders" that the Pharisees observed, particularly in regard to ceremonial washings before meals. And in verses 5–7 we hear about one of the many clashes between them and Jesus over the validity and importance of such rituals:

> The Pharisees and the scribes asked Him, "Why do Your disciples not walk according to the tradition of the elders, but eat their bread with impure hands?" And He said to them, "Rightly did Isaiah prophesy of you hypocrites, as it is written, 'This people honors Me with their lips, but their heart is far away from Me. But in vain do they worship Me, teaching as doctrines the precepts of men.'"

Notice first of all how legalism, or going "beyond what is written," was clearly a problem with the Pharisees. They were upset that the disciples did not obey the tradition of the elders by washing their hands before a meal, a practice that is never actually commanded in the Old Testament. Jesus responded that they were "teaching as doctrines the precepts of men," which along with Paul's words in 1 Corinthians 4:6 is one of the best definitions of legalism in the Bible. But notice also what Jesus says is the result of their going beyond what is written—they had become hypocrites. They were saying something with their lips that was not really true in their hearts, and therefore their worship for God was "vain" or meaningless.

At another time Jesus said, "Beware of the leaven of the Pharisees, which is hypocrisy" (Luke 12:1). That statement equates legalism with hypocrisy, because the two are nearly inseparable. Legalism is a way of *covering* hypocrisy, because it creates external rules that can be kept regardless of the state of the heart—at least in the eyes of others. It allows people to look good outwardly even when their hearts are rotten. But legalism also *causes* hypocrisy, because people learn to keep the external rules without being changed internally. And they also learn to live a life of deceit, in which the way they look to others is more important than how they look to God.

The following story, told by Chuck Swindoll, illustrates some of the connections between legalism and hypocrisy:

> I know a man approaching sixty years of age today who is still haunted by the memory of being raised by hypocritical parents. . . . Throughout his childhood his family attended a church where they were taught you shouldn't go to movies. This was so firmly enforced that in Sunday church services people would be called to come forward to an altar and confess that they had done that or some other "sins." The problem is, his family usually went to movies on Friday or on Saturday night, always in secret. But they made it very clear that he shouldn't say anything about it. They drilled it into him, "Keep your mouth shut." Here he is, a little boy, being lectured on the way home from the theater, week after week, "Don't tell anybody on Sunday that we did this." Of course, they went to see the film miles away from the church so church folks wouldn't know. Not until recently has the man come to realize how damaging that hypocrisy was to his walk with Christ. Because they were not straightforward about the truth, no one should be surprised he picked up a lifestyle of deception and lying.[3]

Of course the same kind of hypocrisy can happen in churches and families where the Word alone is upheld as the standard for spirituality. In other words, people can and do hide *real* sins, not just infractions against human traditions. But there is something about legalism that breeds such hypocrisy in spades. One of the reasons is that extrabiblical "fences" provide a way for people to think that they are righteous when they are really not. In their spiritual pride they are then cut off from the inner work of the Spirit of God, who "is opposed to the proud, but gives grace to the humble" (James 4:6; 1 Peter 5:5). Now they have an overabundance of rules, but no true power within the heart to help them keep the rules, so they learn to fake it. They can't let themselves or anyone else think that they are not right with God, so they deceive themselves and others into thinking that they are. That is why Jesus used such strong words with the legalists of His day (Matt. 23:25–28):

> Woe to you, scribes and Pharisees, hypocrites! For you clean the outside of the cup and of the dish, but inside they are full of robbery and self-indulgence. You blind Pharisee, first clean the inside of the cup and of the dish, so that the outside of it may become clean also.
>
> Woe to you, scribes and Pharisees, hypocrites! For you are like whitewashed tombs which on the outside appear beautiful, but inside they are full of dead men's bones and all uncleanness. So you, too, outwardly appear righteous to men, but inwardly you are full of hypocrisy and lawlessness.

I mentioned that hypocrites often deceive themselves as well as others. Jesus was trying to break through that kind of self-deception with the strong words He used in passages like Matthew 23. He wanted the Pharisees, and anyone like them, to realize that their legalistic attempts to draw closer to God were actually increasing the distance between them and Him. This shows why the gospel of grace is such an important solution to legalism—an idea that we will discuss more in the conclusion of this book. Knowing that God accepts us in Christ keeps us from fabricating human ways to earn acceptance with Him. As Coleman suggests in his book, one of the biggest problems with the Pharisees was that they were basically afraid of God.[4] If only they would have understood how freely His grace is offered to us because of what His Son has done for us, they would not have found it necessary to build fences and add new laws in an attempt to avoid His wrath.

But the Pharisees did not understand and accept God's grace, so there was a shocking inconsistency between their external behavior and their internal quality of character. And they had many more inconsistencies as well, which are shared by others who go beyond what is written. For example, the Word of God applies the same standards to all people, but legalists create rules for others that they do not follow themselves. As Jesus said about the Pharisees, "They tie up heavy burdens, and lay them on men's shoulders, but they themselves are unwilling to move them with so much as a finger" (Matt. 23:4). To use the example of movies again, I remember hearing about a man who was the president of a college where going to movies was forbidden, but he couldn't wait to get out of town so he could go see them. Because pride and legalism are so often related, perhaps he was thinking that he was mature enough to handle it, while almost everyone else was too weak.

Also, the Word of God is divinely inspired and therefore never contradicts itself, but when moral standards of human origin are added to the Word, glaring inconsistencies are inevitable. Still another movie example illustrates this point: At one school I attended, I remember watching Shakespeare's play, *As You Like It*, which was produced and performed by the same faculty who believed it was wrong to go to movies. About halfway through the comedy, which included a cross-dressing hero and numerous innuendos (thinly veiled by the Elizabethan English), it struck me that I had seen basically the same thing that summer, when I had watched the movie *Tootsie*, starring Dustin Hoffman. But that school would never have considered showing *Tootsie* to the student body, presumably because it was cinema rather than live theater, and because it wasn't four hundred years old. Likewise, I noticed a troubling inconsistency when it came to that school's approach to women. They were only allowed to wear dresses, on the one hand, but the faculty wives were required to work on campus and have their young children in daycare. So they were very strict when it came to defining modesty, but looser than many would be in regard to the responsibility of women to be "workers at home" (Titus 2:5).

Another example of glaring inconsistency in a legalist is a young man I once knew who believed that women had to obey men in all circumstances, even if they were told to sin. But on the other hand, he drank very heavily and rationalized that practice by saying that it was a sin only if he hurt somebody—his definition of "dissipation" in Ephesians 5:18. Many more examples could be adduced, of course, but hopefully these are enough to help you see how going beyond what is written produces numerous forms of hypocrisy.

Neglect of the Word

Jesus continues His denouncement of the Pharisees in Mark 7:8–9 by saying, " 'Neglecting the commandment of God, you hold to the tradition of men.' He was also saying to them, 'You are experts at setting aside the commandment of God in order to keep your tradition.' " And in verse 13 He says that they were "invalidating the word of God by your tradition which you have handed down; and you do many things such as that." So according to our Lord, adding to the Word of God actually subtracts from it. We cannot go beyond what is written without in some way detracting from the purity and power of the Scriptures.

There are many reasons why this is true, but the most obvious one is that we don't need to search the Scriptures for guidance when we already have extrabiblical rules that tell us what to do. We don't need the Spirit of God to give us wisdom in applying the principles of the Word when man-made preferences have already settled the issue for us. But though the fences and new laws of the Pharisees might make some decisions easier for God's people, they also make us weaker, because they cut us off from the Word and Spirit, which are the real sources of spiritual power.

Chuck Swindoll illustrates this danger well:

> Someone on our staff at our Insight for Living office informed me several months ago that a woman had called the ministry office to find out what my "official position" was on a certain gray area. When she was told that it's not my policy to make "official" public statements on such issues, she was bewildered . . . actually, a little irritated. She asked, "How are we to know what to decide on this issue if Chuck doesn't tell us?" Some may find her question amusing. Frankly, I find it a little frightening. I thought, "Have we created that kind of Christian, where the minister must make statements in areas that are a matter of personal preference?" There is a fine line between responsible leadership and dogmatic control. All risks notwithstanding, people need to be informed, and then released to come to their own convictions. Why must a

minister constantly issue public edicts and decrees? Seems awfully popelike to me. Have we wandered that far from grace?[5]

Then Swindoll adds some important pastorly advice: "You will never grow up so long as you must get your lists and form most of your opinions from me or some other Christian leader."[6] That advice summarizes the way in which legalism "invalidates" the Word of God, or causes us to neglect it. We will never grow in our knowledge and application of Scripture if we are focused on creating and keeping rules that are outside of it. Put another way, we will never learn to be dependent on and directed by the Spirit of God when we allow men or movements to take the place of the Holy Spirit by telling us how to live the Christian life.

To illustrate how legalism produces a neglect of the Word, Jesus gives an example in Mark 7:10–13:

> For Moses said, "Honor your father and your mother"; and, "He who speaks evil of father or mother, is to be put to death"; but you say, "If a man says to his father or his mother, whatever I have that would help you is Corban (that is to say, given to God)," you no longer permit him to do anything for his father or his mother; thus invalidating the word of God by your tradition which you have handed down.

"Corban" was a tradition of the Jews (not an Old Testament command) by which a man would commit a portion of his wealth to support the temple and priesthood. The Jewish leaders would hold him to this commitment, even if his parents became infirmed and needed that money to survive. So they were placing their man-made policies on a higher level than the Scriptures, which said that we must honor our parents who have cared for us for so many years. In fact, this legalistic rule *prevented* people from obeying the clear teaching of the Bible. And Jesus said, "You do many things such as that" (v. 13).

Some of those "many things" were related to the observance of the Sabbath, an issue that Jesus repeatedly confronted in the Gospels, and one that falls squarely into this discussion of legalistic rules that keep people from living out the commands and principles of Scripture. God had simply told the Jews to make the Sabbath a special time of worship, and to take the day off from work (Exod. 20:8–11). But in their oral and written tradition, they had added to those two commands innumerable fences to keep people from breaking them. One commentator gives us some of the more extreme examples:

> Throwing an object into the air with one hand and catching it with the other was prohibited. If the Sabbath overtook you as you reached for some food, the food was to be dropped before drawing your arm back, lest you be guilty of carrying a burden.
>
> Tailors did not carry a needle with them on the Sabbath for fear they might be tempted to mend a garment and thereby perform work. Nothing could be bought or sold, and clothing could not be dyed or washed. A letter could not be dispatched, even if by the hand of a Gentile. . . .
>
> Baths could not be taken for fear some of the water might spill onto the floor and "wash" it. Chairs could not be moved because dragging them might make a furrow in the ground, and a woman was not to look in a mirror lest she see a gray hair and be tempted to pull it out. You could carry ink enough to draw only two letters of the alphabet, and false teeth could not be worn because they exceeded the weight limit for burdens.[7]

Time and time again, Jesus came into conflict with the Jewish leaders over their perspective on the Sabbath. The book of Luke alone contains numerous passages about this issue, but the first one recorded in that book should suffice to show us why this issue was important to Christ. Luke 6:1–11 reveals two reasons why extrabiblical traditions, like the Jewish Sabbath rules, should never be allowed to become moral standards for the people of God.

First, *extrabiblical traditions will keep you from receiving good things.* Luke 6:1–2 says that on a Sabbath day "His disciples were picking the heads of grain, rubbing them in their hands, and eating the grain. But some of the Pharisees said, 'Why do you do what is not lawful on the Sabbath?' " Notice first of all that the Pharisees thought that the disciples were breaking the law, even though the Old Testament law never spoke against what they were doing. So obviously these legalists had elevated their traditions to the level of Scripture. But Jesus did not zero in on that distinction, though He could have. Instead He talked about how David and his companions had eaten the consecrated bread in the tabernacle when they were hungry, even though the tradition had said that only priests were to eat that bread.

This passage has some deeper meanings that are outside the purview of this discussion, like David's being a picture of Christ and Christ's being "Lord of the Sabbath" (v. 5), and thus able to change Sabbath law if He desired. But regarding the issue of legalism, Jesus' response clearly indicates that He wanted the disciples to enjoy some good food on that day, and He was not about to let the Jewish traditions keep them from it. Likewise, the Lord wants us to enjoy good things today as well, and we should not allow unbiblical rules and regulations to stop us, unless they would cause our brother to sin (see next chapter). It seems

Jesus and Legalism

to me that this would apply to various forms of recreation, like relaxing after a tough week by watching a football game on Sunday, as long it does not take the place of worshipping with God's people. After all, different people "rest" in different ways! And as passages like Ecclesiastes 11:9 and 1 Corinthians 7:39 indicate, we have freedom to follow our desires in areas that the Scripture does not address.[8]

An even bigger problem, however, is that *extrabiblical traditions will keep you from doing good things.* Luke 6:6–11 tells the story of a Sabbath healing, the first of many that Jesus performed, even though He knew the Jewish leaders would hate Him for it:

> On another Sabbath He entered the synagogue and was teaching; and there was a man there whose right hand was withered. The scribes and the Pharisees were watching Him closely to see if He healed on the Sabbath, so that they might find reason to accuse Him. But He knew what they were thinking, and He said to the man with the withered hand, "Get up and come forward!" And he got up and came forward. And Jesus said to them, "I ask you, is it lawful to do good or to do harm on the Sabbath, to save a life or to destroy it?" After looking around at them all, He said to him, "Stretch out your hand!" And he did so; and his hand was restored. But they themselves were filled with rage, and discussed together what they might do to Jesus.

If our Lord would have followed the traditions of His culture, He would not have healed that man on the Sabbath. But He was more concerned with *doing* good than He was with *looking* good. So He stood up to the religious bullies of the day and broke their traditions right in front of them, to set an example for us (see also Luke 13:10–17 and 14:1–6). To be like our Lord Jesus, we must be careful that we do not allow rules that are not based on the clear teaching of Scripture to keep us from doing good things.

An obvious application today, related to the Sabbath, is that we should not judge Christians who work on Sundays in service occupations, like doctors or firemen (both of which we have in our church, by the way). But I also think it is wrong to judge people who enjoy some form of recreation with their children when they have little opportunity for that on other days—as long as they have made corporate worship a priority.

And even watching football can become an opportunity for service. I have a friend who refused for many years to watch any sports on Sundays, but after he was challenged to study further and could not find anything in the Bible about it, he accepted an invitation to watch the Super Bowl at a friend's house. And he had an opportunity that night to share the gospel with a non-Christian who was also attending the party. It seems to me that anyone who looks down on my friend for doing that would be a little too much like the Pharisees who couldn't appreciate the healing of a cripple on the Sabbath. And what if my friend would decide to make a weekly ministry out of watching football with nonbelievers on Sunday, so he could build bridges for the gospel? Would we want to say this is wrong, and hinder him from that ministry? Or should we say that it's okay, as long as he doesn't drink any beer with them?

All kidding aside, I want to challenge you to think through this issue, and any other similar ones you may face, with the words and actions of Jesus firmly in mind. Make sure that you have the same skepticism that He had toward man-made rules, and make sure that you never set aside the commandment of God in order to keep your tradition.

False Spirituality

The third dangerous result of legalism that Jesus addresses in Mark 7 is a wrong approach to spiritual life and growth, which actually hinders us from growing in Christ. As our Lord indicates in Mark 7:14–16, going beyond what is written produces *an overemphasis on the external, to the exclusion of the internal*: "After He called the crowd to Him again, He began saying to them, 'Listen to Me, all of you, and understand: there is nothing outside the man which can defile him if it goes into him; but the things which proceed out of the man are what defile the man. If anyone has ears to hear, let him hear.' "

In the following verses (17–23), Jesus basically repeats the same idea in an expanded form. Why does He take so much time and effort to make this point, that it is not evil from the outside that defiles us, but evil from the inside? The answer is that legalism gets this point precisely backwards. Legalism builds fences to keep sin away from us, or to keep us away from sin, but often fails to address the sin that we carry *with us* at all times inside our hearts. This is one reason that we are so easily drawn toward legalism, because it provides an easy way to be spiritual, or at least to be considered spiritual by others. It is easier to stay away from the movie theater than it is to have a transformed heart that loves good and hates evil when we see it. It is easier to follow someone's rules about parenting than it is to genuinely love and fervently pray for our children. As Carl Henry wrote, "One who abstains from the prescribed may be every bit as carnal as one who indulges. Arbitrary legalism is a poor substitute for inner morality. Not only this, but such legalism emphasizes the less important issues in life, and ignores or excuses the weightier matters of the Law. Smoking can be a subject of legislation; pride cannot."[9]

That quote alludes to another passage in the Gospels where the false spirituality of the Pharisees is exposed. In Matthew 23:23–24 Jesus says, "Woe to you, scribes and Pharisees, hypocrites! For you tithe mint and dill and cummin, and have neglected the weightier provisions of the law: justice and mercy and faithfulness; but these are the things you should have done without neglecting the others. You blind guides, who strain out a gnat and swallow a camel!" Legalistic individuals and environments tend to be characterized by a preoccupation with relatively insignificant issues, while some of the more important aspects of Christian living are sadly neglected. This reminds us of Paul's words about extrabiblical rules in Colossians 2:23, which we discussed in chapter 5: "These are matters which have, to be sure, the appearance of wisdom . . . , but are of no value against fleshly indulgence." A legalistic approach to spirituality simply does not make you more godly—even though you may appear to be—because it cannot change your heart.

The example of fasting. In Mark 7 Jesus addresses the issue of food when He tells us that it is not what we put into our bodies that defiles us. At another point in His ministry, however, He found Himself in a dispute with the Pharisees over what they did *not* put into their bodies. Luke 5:33–37 says:

> And they said to Him, "The disciples of John often fast and offer prayers, the disciples of the Pharisees also do the same, but Yours eat and drink." And Jesus said to them, "You cannot make the attendants of the bridegroom fast while the bridegroom is with them, can you? But the days

will come; and when the bridegroom is taken away from them, then they will fast in those days." And He was also telling them a parable: "No one tears a piece of cloth from a new garment and puts it on an old garment; otherwise he will both tear the new, and the piece from the new will not match the old. And no one puts new wine into old wineskins; otherwise the new wine will burst the skins and it will be spilled out, and the skins will be ruined."

The Jews had developed a system of regular fasts that they thought would bring them closer to God. But it is interesting to note that this practice did not come from the Old Testament. In fact, there was only one day during each year that the law required the people of Israel to fast, and that was the Day of Atonement.[10] And since there is no command to fast in the New Testament, and the Day of Atonement has been fulfilled in Christ, I think it is safe to say that fasting is not a biblical requirement for Christians. Furthermore, Jesus implies in that passage that fasting is an infrequent and almost involuntary response to some great hardship or challenge that we face in our lives (v. 35; cf. Matt. 17:21). And finally, the epistles refer to the practice of abstaining from food in a negative way, not a positive way (1 Tim. 4:3). But yet there are many Christians today, and even many Christian leaders, who advocate fasting as a spiritual discipline that supposedly will bring you closer to God. They advocate practicing it regularly, even though it was the Pharisees, and *not* Jesus and His disciples, who did that in Bible times!

Fasting in itself, for health or weight-loss purposes, is not wrong. But it seems to me that treating it like a kind of sacrament goes directly against the point of Jesus' teaching, especially the parable of the new wineskins in the passage above. The point of that parable is that our Lord's New Covenant teaching is simply not compatible with the old Jewish traditions, and that the two cannot be mixed without some damage being done to the truth. Likewise, we must be careful not to mix the true, biblical spirituality of the heart with the externalism of nonbiblical methods of growth.

The example of the Sabbath. Jesus was concerned about the way His people viewed the Sabbath because they were missing the main point. We find a hint of this concern when we hear Jesus saying, "The Sabbath was made for man, and not man for the Sabbath" (Mark 2:27). But we get the full picture when we understand that the command to rest on the Sabbath was given as a picture of our spiritual rest from our self-righteousness and self-rule, a rest that we enjoy in Christ. In his book *Calvin and the Sabbath*, Richard Gaffin quotes the great Genevan Reformer as saying, "Though the ceremonies and outward rite have been abolished, . . . we still retain the truth of the precept, that the Lord willed the Jews and us to have forever and in common."[11] Then Gaffin explains:

> What is this truth? First, that we should enter into the spiritual rest provided by Christ. That means that we must cease from our own sinful works and rest in God, letting Him, by the Holy Spirit, work in us. To submit to the dominion of the Holy Spirit is to obey the fourth commandment. "All works of this sort are servile. From them the law of the Sabbath bids us cease, that God may dwell in us, may effect what is good, and rule us by the leading of the Holy Spirit, whose kingdom imparts peace and tranquility to the conscience."[12]

How ironic that the Pharisees, who were so concerned about the details of keeping the Sabbath, had developed a system of works righteousness that violated the basic purpose of that commandment! By going beyond what is written, they ended up straining out a gnat and swallowing a camel, clinging stubbornly to a host of meaningless extrabiblical traditions but forfeiting the wonderful saving truths that the Sabbath signified.

Now you can see why Jesus would intentionally stir up controversy by introducing the Sabbath issue into a conversation, and then breaking His opponents' rules right in front of them by healing a man on the Sabbath (see Luke 14:1–6). He realized that it was important for His people to identify and avoid all forms of legalism, because otherwise they would fall prey to problems like hypocrisy, neglect of the Word, and false spirituality. He wants us to be able to run the race that is set before us, and He knows that to do so we must first lay aside every encumbrance that might be holding us back (Heb. 12:1).

Questions for Discussion and Application

1. How would you define "hypocrisy"? How is it related to legalism?
2. Why do you think Christians tend to look to a respected leader to tell them what they should do and not do in their lives? What are the dangers of this tendency?
3. What are some Pharisaic fences that people today have erected to keep themselves and others from sinning? Do they really work in the end? Why or why not?
4. What do you think about this statement: "Recovery groups like AA are preoccupied with whether or not you drink, but the more important issue is *why* you drink."

What to Do When Someone Is Different from You

D ifferences between people provide the occasion for the problems of judging and legalism. We are tempted to judge others because they are doing something that we would not do (or at least that we are not doing at the time). We become prideful and divided against one another because of legalistic rules that may work fine for one Christian, but not for another. Whole groups of Christians become suspicious and cynical of other groups, basically because we are different from one another. But these things do not ever need to happen, because the Lord has given us a wealth of instruction in the Scriptures about how to relate to others who have different perspectives and practices.

In fact, two entire chapters of the New Testament are devoted to this issue—Romans 14 and 1 Corinthians 8. Romans 14 itself is so clear and complete that one wonders why we ever have conflicts on nonbiblical issues when God has instructed us so well on the matter. And we will never have them again, if we understand the principles taught in this great chapter and apply them by the power of the Holy Spirit. We will also learn the answers to many of the questions that may be in your mind after reading this far in the book. The apostle Paul was writing to people who had struggles similar to the ones we face, and his inspired words illuminate our times as well.

The primary issue that Romans 14 addresses is the eating of meat from animals that had been offered to idols in the pagan temples, then sold in the marketplace as food. Some Christians thought that it was fine to buy and enjoy such meat, because they were not worshipping the false gods to whom the animals had been offered. They were simply enjoying some good food, for which they thanked God. Other Christians, however, believed that it was a sin to buy and eat such meat, because they saw it as a form of participation in the idolatry of the temples. "You're giving money to an ungodly system that is abhorrent to God," they would say, "and you are associating yourself with it by enjoying something that comes from it." In addition to that concern, there were undoubtedly some Christians who believed that evil spirits from the false worship inhabited the meat itself, and so anyone who ate it would be spiritually contaminated.

What you need to understand at the beginning of this discussion, so you can understand the rest of it, is that the second group was clearly wrong in their perspective on the activity. Paul says in Romans 14:14, "I know and am convinced that nothing is unclean in itself," and in other passages about the same topic he says repeatedly, "All things are lawful to me" (1 Cor. 6:12; 10:23). What he means by that statement is that all things that are not unlawful are lawful—in other words, if the Word of God doesn't say it is wrong, then it is not wrong in itself. And God had never said it was wrong to eat meat offered to idols, so for at least some Christians, it was an acceptable thing to do.[1]

But knowing that fact alone does not solve the problem. We still have the problem that some Christians *believe* it is wrong to eat the meat, and so they would be going against their conscience to do so. Should they eat the meat anyway, even though they think it is wrong? And what responsibility do the other Christians have to help them in this regard? And finally, how can both groups resist the temptation to judge and divide from one another? Those are the kinds of questions Paul answers in Romans 14, as he teaches us four principles that we can apply whenever we encounter people who are different from us in their views of issues not addressed in the Scriptures. You can plug any such issue into this discussion and it will apply. Instead of meat offered to idols, you can read this chapter with movies in mind, or drinking, or dancing, or music, or worship styles, or education choices, or whatever other issue that may be controversial among Christians, but has not been clearly settled by the Word of God. By understanding Paul's inspired words in Romans 14, and other related passages, you will know how to think and act in regard to all such issues.

The Principle of Acceptance

Paul begins his discussion of disputable matters by telling us that we need to accept one another, even though we may have different perspectives, and be careful not to judge one another. Romans 14:1–4 says:

> Now accept the one who is weak in faith, but not for the purpose of passing judgment on his opinions. One person has faith that he may eat all things, but he who is weak eats vegetables only. The one who eats is not to regard with contempt the one who does not eat, and the one who does not eat is not to judge the one who eats, for God has accepted him. Who are you to judge the servant of another? To his

own master he stands or falls; and he will stand, for the Lord is able to make him stand.

When Paul says, "accept the one who is weak in faith" (v. 1), he is referring to a person who is not able to do what you may be able to do with a clear conscience. He is not talking about saving faith here, nor is he saying that the person is a weaker person in general, nor is he even saying that he has less faith in God than anyone else does. Paul uses "faith" here to speak of the belief or confidence that something we are doing is right. That is why in verse 2 he says, "One person has faith that he may eat all things, but he who is weak eats vegetables only." First Corinthians 8:7 and 8:12, a passage that discusses the same issue of meat offered to idols, helps us to understand this when it refers to someone's *conscience* being "weak." Christians are "weak" in a particular area when God allows freedom in that area, but they are restricted by their conscience and therefore cannot enjoy that freedom.

After informing us about these inevitable differences among Christians, Paul says we must not judge one another in the sinful sense that we have already discussed in this book. He knows that when differences like this occur, we are most tempted to look on each other "with contempt" (Rom. 14:3). The person who can enjoy the meat with a clear conscience is likely to view the weaker brother as immature, over-traditional, not living in grace, or legalistic (even though he may not be foisting his practice on others). On the other hand, the one who cannot eat the meat with a good conscience will tend to judge the one who does as immature, worldly, loose, unconcerned with holiness, and so on. But notice that Paul repeats the same concept twice in verses 3–4: "God has accepted him," and "he will stand, for the Lord is able to make him stand."

Both the one who eats, and the one who doesn't, are acceptable to God if they are motivated by pleasing Him. So we must not "judge the servant of another."

One of the reasons that it is so important to understand what Paul means by "weak" is that we must remember that we are all weak in one way or another, and this will help us to treat others with grace. We all have areas of our lives in which our conscience restricts us, areas in which we will be tempted to judge others. For instance, Tom might be tempted to judge Jerry because Jerry listens to rock music, goes to movies, and doesn't like to wear ties. But at the very same time, Jerry might be tempted to judge Tom as materialistic because he drives a Mercedes, unspiritual because he has not studied important Bible doctrines, and vain because he dresses up so often! They will be friends, and brothers who can serve together, only when they learn to accept one another on these extrabiblical issues. They can and should challenge one another in a humble way, even concerning those issues, but they must be careful to not cross the line into sinful judging and legalism.

The Principle of Personal Conviction

Romans 14:5 says, "One person regards one day above another, another regards every day alike. Each person must be fully convinced in his own mind." Here Paul introduces another controversial issue among Christians of the day— the observance of the Sabbath, which we discussed in chapter 7.[2] But his point applies to all such issues when he says, "Each person must be fully convinced in his own mind." God wants us to give thoughtful and prayerful consideration to these matters, until we have developed a personal conviction based on careful study, godly counsel, and even vigorous debate.

Notice the emphasis on being "fully convinced in his *own* mind," however. This verse is not saying that we should develop a conviction that applies to everybody else, which on nonbiblical issues would be legalism. Rather he is saying that we should decide what *we will practice personally*, in our own lives and families. This distinction is crucial and lies at the heart of how we can get along with those who are different. It is very right and biblical to say, "This is my personal conviction, but I respect the different convictions of others on this matter."

What would not be right and biblical, however, would be to say, "I have freedom, so don't judge me" on issues that we have not carefully considered. It is too easy for us to choose the path that we want to walk, and then simply claim freedom to do so, when in fact that might not be the right way to go. That is why Paul says, "Each person must be *fully convinced* in his own mind." And he adds in Galatians 5:13, "You were called to freedom, brethren; only do not turn your freedom into an opportunity for the flesh." The only way to avoid this kind of careless libertinism is to do some hard work in study, prayer, and counsel before you decide what you will do in regard to controversial issues.

And how will you know if you have reached a godly personal conviction, and have true freedom from the Lord in this area? You will know when you are able to *give thanks to God* for what you are doing, and when you can honestly say that you are doing it *for the glory of God*, and when you are ready to answer for it *at the judgment of God*. This is what Paul teaches in the next section, Romans 14:6–12:

> He who observes the day, observes it for the Lord, and he
> who eats, does so for the Lord, for he gives thanks to God;
> and he who eats not, for the Lord he does not eat, and gives

thanks to God. For not one of us lives for himself, and not one dies for himself; for if we live, we live for the Lord, or if we die, we die for the Lord; therefore whether we live or die, we are the Lord's. For to this end Christ died and lived again, that He might be Lord both of the dead and of the living.

But you, why do you judge your brother? Or you again, why do you regard your brother with contempt? For we shall all stand before the judgment seat of God. For it is written, "As I live, says the Lord, every knee shall bow to Me, and every tongue shall give praise to God." So then each one of us will give an account of himself to God.

In light of this passage, I encourage you to examine the choices you have made about controversial issues that are not directly addressed in the Scriptures. Ask yourself these questions about them: Can I give thanks to God for what I am doing, or is it something I'd rather not talk to Him about? (Or if it is something I choose not to do, can I thank God for that without sounding like the Pharisee in Luke 18:11?) Am I really doing this *for the Lord*, and for His glory, or is it merely a selfish desire that in no way contributes to my relationship with Him? And is this something I will be ashamed about when I stand before the Lord? Or if He were sitting next to me right now, would I be doing this?

Those questions will help you to form good personal convictions, and plan ahead of time how you will act, rather than just falling into whatever practice feels right at the time. I suggest that you not make vows to the Lord about matters outside of Scripture, however, because your perspective might change at some time in the future, and you don't want to be locked into something that might not be the best (see Eccl. 5:4–7). But until your convictions change for good reason, follow them consistently for the glory of God, and be careful not to judge others who have different ones.

The Principle of Edification

Even when we have freedom before God in particular areas of our lives, we may sometimes need to restrict our freedom for the purpose of building up our brothers and sisters in Christ. This is because God does not want anyone to act against his conscience (see the next section), and we must be careful not to tempt anyone to do so. Paul explains all this in Romans 14:13–21:

> Therefore let us not judge one another anymore, but rather determine this—not to put an obstacle or a stumbling block in a brother's way. I know and am convinced in the Lord Jesus that nothing is unclean in itself; but to him who thinks anything to be unclean, to him it is unclean. For if because of food your brother is hurt, you are no longer walking according to love. Do not destroy with your food him for whom Christ died. Therefore do not let what is for you a good thing be spoken of as evil; for the kingdom of God is not eating and drinking, but righteousness and peace and joy in the Holy Spirit. For he who in this way serves Christ is acceptable to God and approved by men. So then we pursue the things which make for peace and the building up of one another. Do not tear down the work of God for the sake of food. All things indeed are clean, but they are evil for the man who eats and gives offense. It is good not to eat meat or to drink wine, or to do anything by which your brother stumbles.

There are times when it is not right to enjoy your liberty in Christ, because doing so would be harmful to another Christian (cf. 1 Cor. 8:4–13). Others who think what you are doing is wrong might choose to do it also, because they feel pressure to be like you, or because their flesh will use your actions as an excuse to act against their conscience. Whatever the reason, that would be a sinful choice on their part, which would impair their relationship with God (Rom. 14:14, 23—we will learn why this is true in the next section). So we need to be aware of the weaknesses of other Christians, as much as possible, and be careful to act in a way that edifies them rather than encourages them to sin. As Paul adds in Romans 15:1–2, "We who are strong ought to bear the weaknesses of those without strength and not just please ourselves. Each of us is to please his neighbor for his good, to his edification."

One time I was playing Uno® with three of my children. The youngest one, Madison, was only four and still learning how to win and lose with grace. So when things were not going her way in the game, she would be tempted to whine and cry. In one particular game, she was not doing well at all, and she was on the edge of losing it. I, on the other hand, was about to win, and I almost put down a "Draw Four" card which would have put her deeper into the hole and almost certainly sent her over the edge emotionally. But I didn't want to have to discipline her for throwing a tantrum, and I wanted her to have a good first experience with the game, so I kept the "Draw Four" card in my hand and picked one off the pile (which disadvantaged me, of course). Then the next time around, the only card I could play was the "Draw Four," but after staring for a moment into her gorgeous blue eyes and noticing her quivering lip, I kept it in my hand and drew again. This happened a third time, and a fourth time, until Maddy finally won the game, and I was left with a big stack of cards!

I don't like losing any kind of game, even when the winner is so cute, but I thought afterwards what a great illustration that is of how we should treat one another in the body of Christ. We must be willing to give up our rights to keep others from going down the wrong path, when we know they might be headed that way.

I have not taken a vow to lose every game I ever play, however. This will serve to correct a misunderstanding that some people have of the principle of edification. I've heard Christians say that no one should ever drink alcohol, for instance, because some people are addicted and cannot handle it. If our actions *might possibly* cause someone to stumble in that or any area, they say, then we should abstain at all times, just in case. But the first problem with that idea is that if we were to apply it consistently, we would become catatonic zombies who never do anything! We shouldn't go to a mall, because a lot of people struggle with covetousness and materialism. We shouldn't eat food, because gluttony and obesity are such common problems. And we wouldn't want to brush our teeth or tame our hair, because someone somewhere might possibly be led into vanity!

The other problem with that approach, however, is that it is simply not scriptural. Paul gives some further instruction in 1 Corinthians 10:23–29, which makes it clear that he is not talking about abstaining from all meat, or even all meat offered to idols. He is dealing with a situational issue that requires a situational application:

> All things are lawful, but not all things are profitable. All things are lawful, but not all things edify. Let no one seek his own good, but that of his neighbor. Eat anything that

is sold in the meat market without asking questions for conscience' sake; for the earth is the Lord's, and all it contains. If one of the unbelievers invites you and you want to go, eat anything that is set before you without asking questions for conscience' sake. But if anyone says to you, "This is meat sacrificed to idols," do not eat it, for the sake of the one who informed you, and for conscience' sake; I mean not your own conscience, but the other man's.

In this passage Paul repeats the principle of edification, but he also makes clear that he is talking about applying it in situations where we *know* that our potential actions will cause a brother or sister to sin. If we have no reason to think that will occur, Paul says, then we can go ahead and enjoy our freedom in Christ. So applying the principle today to something like drinking would mean that if you know someone is struggling with alcohol addiction, and he or she will be tempted to drink because you are doing so, then you should abstain in that circumstance. Or if a certain kind of music brings back memories of a former lifestyle, and tempts someone to sin, then you should not listen to it around him or her. But if no such issue is raised, you can go ahead and listen (if you can give thanks to God and do it for His glory).[3]

Another common misconception relates to the meaning of the word "offense." Because we use that word in the sense of offending someone, or bothering someone by our actions, it is easy to read that idea into texts like Romans 14:20. We might think that we should not do anything that bothers other Christians, including judgmental people with a legalistic viewpoint. But that is not what Paul means here when he refers to "giving offense"—he is referring to causing someone to sin (an older and less common meaning of the term). On the contrary, Jesus had no qualms about bothering judgmental people like the Pharisees—in fact, He sometimes went out of His way to do it (see Luke 14:1–5 again).

Here we need to recognize an important distinction between "weaker brothers" and "Pharisees," which Garry Friesen explains well:

> In all, there are three categories of differing Christians to whom we must properly relate. The believer who is correctly responding to biblical guidelines in debatable areas is a *convinced differing brother.* I am to accept him and refrain from judging him for his opinions, as he is to do for me. The other classification we have discussed is the weaker brother. I am to be alert for him, limiting the exercise of my freedom when my influence might tempt him to sin against his conscience.
>
> There remains a third kind of differing believer that we encounter from time to time. He is the one who does not accept me with my differing convictions; who puts pressure on others to conform to his point of view. In terms of stumbling blocks, he *takes offense* when no offense is *given.* The cause of the offense is his own pride and unbelief, rather than improper behavior on the part of the other. He becomes upset, but is not "destroyed." He is not a weaker brother for he is strong in his convictions and will not blindly follow a contrary example. Nor is he a stronger brother, for he is not strong in understanding. He has not fully grasped the nature and reality of Christian freedom and responsibility, especially as it affects relationships with other Christians.
>
> Though not given the same systematic treatment in Romans and 1 Corinthians as the weaker brother, this third

character appears frequently on the pages of the New Testament. For purposes of terminology, we will employ the title of the classic example to designate this category of debater—the Pharisee.

By way of definition, the Pharisee is *a professing believer with strong convictions who, because of his own pride, takes offense at those who resist his pressure to conform to his point of view.* By his nature, the Pharisee is most in need of the correctives set forth in Romans 14:1–12. Of the three types of differing brothers, he is also the most difficult to get along with.[4]

Jesus did not change His behavior just because the Pharisees might judge Him, because there were bigger issues at stake than making them happy or avoiding their scorn. Likewise, Paul refused to capitulate to pressure from legalistic Christians who were demanding that the Gentiles submit to circumcision before they could be considered equal with the Jews. In Galatians 2:3–5 he writes this about his trip to Jerusalem:

> But not even Titus who was with me, though he was a Greek, was compelled to be circumcised. But it was because of the false brethren secretly brought in, who had sneaked in to spy out our liberty which we have in Christ Jesus, in order to bring us into bondage. But we did not yield in subjection to them for even an hour, so that the truth of the gospel would remain with you.

Paul "did not yield" to the Pharisaical Christians. That they might be "offended" at what he did was not grounds to capitulate. He knew that conforming to their rules would give tacit approval to their harmful practice of going beyond what is written.

The Principle of Conscience

The apostle Paul ends his discussion in Romans 14 by explaining more about Christian liberty and its relation to that mysterious faculty of the human soul that we call the conscience. In verses 22–23 he says, "The faith which you have, have as your own conviction before God. Happy is he who does not condemn himself in what he approves. But he who doubts is condemned if he eats, because his eating is not from faith; and whatever is not from faith is sin."

When Paul talks about "the faith which you have," he is again referring to a belief that something you do is right before God. So he repeats his encouragement to develop personal convictions, but he also may be implying that you should keep some of them to yourself, especially in situations where they may cause sin, or controversy, or anything that might be harmful to other Christians.[5] And then he encourages us to enjoy the freedom we have in Christ, and to enjoy the good things that God has given us, even if others might judge us for it. According to Paul, we are happy or blessed when we do not feel guilty, or think we are sinning, in doing the things that the Lord allows. ("What he approves" is probably a reference to God.)[6]

But then Paul adds an important warning: no one should act against his or her conscience. It is not spiritually healthy to do so, and it is also displeasing to God.[7] He who doubts that what he doing is right, the Scripture says, is condemned if he does it ("condemned" here means guilty, or sinning). From the context, we know that this statement applies even to activities that are not wrong in themselves, like eating meat offered to idols. For we are told that someone who eats meat, or does anything else the Bible does not address, is sinning if he is not sure it is right. How can this be? Well, Paul explains in the second half of the verse:

"because his eating is not from faith: and whatever is not from faith is sin."

If we think something is wrong to do, and we do it anyway, it is a sin—even if God never said that the activity itself is wrong. This is because our choice has not been made because of faith, but because of some other motive. So it is not the action itself, but the choice, that is displeasing to God. A helpful illustration would be a woman who was taught while growing up, by her parents and her church, that wearing pants is wrong. Men wear pants, the argument goes, so women should not wear pants. This is a legalistic view that is read into Scripture (because of the Old Testament prohibition of cross-dressing, perhaps the New Testament passages on modesty), but does not proceed from a sound interpretation of Scripture and is not consistent with common sense.[8] Any idea has a certain power, however, when you hear it over and over again from the people you love and respect, especially when you are a child. So she has been convinced that it is wrong for her to wear pants.

Now suppose she is getting ready to go out for the evening with some female friends, who are all wearing jeans and begin to encourage her to do the same. They even poke fun at her hesitancy, and practically browbeat her into breaking her tradition. If she decides to put the jeans on while she still thinks it might be wrong, she will be sinning, because at that moment something is more important to her than pleasing God. It will not be her faith in Him that motivates her to put those jeans on, but her fear of what her friends think, and perhaps her own comfort. Should her conscience be realigned, or retrained, so that she could wear pants without feeling guilty? Yes, I think it should. But until that happens, she should not wear pants, because doing so will come between her and God. It will damage the most important relationship she has, because when she prays to Him she will not be able to pray "in faith," believing that He hears her. Instead she will be thinking something like this: "I don't know if I should be wearing these pants—God might be upset with me."

Your conscience is like a diagnostic program running at all times on a computer. Depending on the information it has been given, it will judge whether you are doing the right thing or the wrong thing. If it judges that you are doing the wrong thing, it will flash a warning light (we call this "feeling guilty"). That warning light of guilt is very helpful in keeping us from moral crashes, but sometimes a conscience can be *overactive* on a particular issue, because it has been given wrong information. So like a computer, it can be reprogrammed with different and better information, so that it will not set off an alarm when not really necessary. Your ultimate goal should be to have a conscience that is fully informed by Scripture, which will keep you from doing only that which is displeasing to God, and not from doing the good things you have the freedom to enjoy.

So your conscience may need to be retrained on a particular issue or issues, but as long as you think something is wrong, don't do it. Because if you act against your conscience repeatedly, then you will develop what the Bible calls a "seared conscience" (see 1 Tim. 4:2; Titus 1:15; Eph. 4:19). In such a conscience, the warning light has been ignored so often that it no longer flashes, and we find ourselves blind and enslaved to sins that will eventually destroy us. As Proverbs 14:12 and 16:25 say, "There is a way which seems right to a man, but its end is the way of death."

So the old saying, "Let your conscience be your guide," is not entirely true. Your conscience can be wrong, and may need to be retrained, as in the case of the woman who cannot wear pants. But though your conscience should not be your *guide* in determining the truth, it should be your *guard* in the sense that it can keep you from wrong paths that lead to destruction. We should never push past this guard, but sometimes we might persuade it through biblical reasoning to move out of the way. On the other hand, we need to be constantly arming our conscience with more principles from Scripture, so it can protect us from choices that would hurt us in the end.

Questions for Discussion and Application

1. What are some activities today that some Christians think are okay, and other Christians do not? Which of these are addressed in the Scriptures, and which are not?
2. Are you friends with other Christians who have convictions different from yours, or are your relationships basically confined to people who are like you?
3. Think of something you do that other Christians might judge you for. Have you studied that issue thoroughly in the Scriptures, heard the other side with an open mind, and sought counsel from mature people on the matter? If not, plan to do those things so you can be "fully convinced in your own mind."
4. What are some examples in your life of how you have restricted your own liberty for the sake of a weaker brother?
5. Is there any area of your life in which you do not have a clear conscience before the Lord? If so, what will be the consequences if you continue to act against your conscience?

CHAPTER NINE

Case Study 1: Entertainment and the Popular Arts

How can we avoid the problem of going "beyond what is written" in regard to others, but still find our own solutions to the difficult ethical choices we face as Christians? To better understand the answer to that question, it would be helpful to take an in-depth look at one of the issues that presents great difficulty in our contemporary culture—one that has also been the occasion for much judgmentalism and legalism in the church.

What kinds of movies, television programs, music, novels, etc., can a Christian enjoy, and still be honoring to God? No other issue has been the source of more friction between Christians in our media-soaked, pleasure-worshipping society, and no other issue has given rise to so many legalistic rules in an attempt to keep us from being contaminated by the world. Some Christians say we should avoid movies altogether; others say only G-rated ones are acceptable. Some say no secular music is good to listen to; others add "Christian contemporary" as a taboo because it sounds too much like what unbelievers are producing. On every issue in this general category, many Christians are far too loose in their practice, but on the other hand, many others overreact to the dangers of modern media by setting up rules that "go beyond what is written," and are therefore susceptible to all the dangers described in this book. So how can we understand this issue in a way that avoids the extremes and maintains a biblical balance?

A Matter of the Heart

First, we need to understand that the Bible offers very few specific rules about this issue, if any, and therefore we should not expect to find easy answers that apply to everyone. It is mostly an individual matter of "the heart"—a term which in the Bible means our "inner man," where we think, desire, worship, and make choices ("mind" and "will" are aspects of the heart).[1] In Mark 7:18–21 Jesus says that "whatever goes into the man from outside cannot defile him, . . . that which proceeds out of the man, that is what defiles the man." He then goes on to say evil comes "from within, out of the heart." What we take into our eyes and ears can certainly *tempt* or *influence* us, as we will discuss, but it cannot necessarily cause us to sin. So the response of our hearts to what we see and hear is the ultimate issue in morality. This is very important to understand, in order to avoid legalism in this matter. An activity that might be wrong for one person might be right for another, depending on what is happening in their hearts.

Some Christians, either in creed or merely in practice, advocate a rejection of any kind of artistic expression and enjoyment. But that approach is clearly inconsistent with Scripture. As T. M. Moore points out:

> Anyone who reads the Bible, paying careful attention not only to the words of the text but also the *forms* of God's revelation, will be struck by the widespread and varied use of the arts for communicating God's purposes and will. The Old and New Testaments alike make abundant use of the

arts: visual arts (the Tabernacle and Temple and all their decorations, the pillar of memorial stones on the banks of the Jordan); musical arts (psalms and spiritual songs); literary arts (story-telling, poetry, perhaps even drama, all kinds of metaphors and images); and a wide variety of abstract and visionary art forms (the first chapters of Ezekiel and Revelation, for example).[2]

We could add to that list the fact that the apostle Paul seems to have enjoyed reading the Greek poets, because he quoted from them in his message on Mars Hill in Acts 17:28. And to mention a different but related issue, he also seems to have been a spectator at the Greek Olympics and other sporting events of his time, because he makes frequent reference to them in his letters (e.g., 1 Cor. 9:24–27; Heb. 12:1–2).[3]

So there is nothing inherently wrong with any of the art forms that people enjoy today, and there is nothing wrong with *enjoying* them, even as mere entertainment. This is important to discuss because some Christians point out that the Bible does not mention entertainment, and therefore infer that it is somehow a questionable concept. But of course the Bible does not mention pizza or toothbrushes either, and that does not make those things bad. And the Bible does contain the idea of entertainment, if not the word itself. One of the themes of the book of Ecclesiastes, for instance, is that God wants you to "enjoy life" (Eccl. 9:9) when it is centered on Him. He tells us to "eat, drink, and be merry" several times in the book (5:18; 8:15; 9:7), and to "follow the impulses of your heart and the desires of your eyes" (11:9).

The reference to eating and drinking is especially helpful in understanding how God wants us to enjoy ourselves (in moderation, of course). Some of the food and drink He has given us, and some of the eating and drinking we do, are merely for utilitarian purposes, to nourish our bodies. But beyond that He has blessed us with *enjoyable* food and drink, and we partake sometimes merely for the pure pleasure of it, not simply to keep ourselves alive. And this is according to His design—just as He has designed the arts for our enjoyment, as well as for our edification.

Most Christians will admit that modern forms of entertainment are not sinful in themselves, and that they can be used by believers for godly purposes. But many have a problem with anything produced by unbelievers, because it almost always contains ideas that are contrary to God's Word and depictions of behavior that God has forbidden. In addition, unbelieving artists often live very ungodly lifestyles. We must remember, however, that unbelievers can indeed produce things that are acceptable and helpful to Christians. This is obvious in the scientific realm, of course, because we benefit from the medical and technological skills of unbelievers all the time. But it is also true in the realm of the arts, as evidenced by Paul's use of the work of Greek poets, which I mentioned above. Most Christians can appreciate the music of Mozart and Tchaikovsky, for example, even though one was a libertine and the other a homosexual. So why can we not enjoy the good work of modern-day artists, even though they may not be godly themselves?

The book of Ecclesiastes is again helpful in this regard, because it says that to His people God "has given wisdom and knowledge and joy, while to the sinner He has given the task of gathering and collecting so that he may give to one who is good in God's sight" (Eccl. 2:26). The abilities that unbelievers have, including their cinematic, musical, and literary skills, have been given to them by God so that they can produce art that can be beneficial and enjoyable to Christians. This does not mean that *all* the art or entertainment produced by the world is for Christians to enjoy, but it is certainly reasonable to assume that *some* of it is.

Those who tell believers to stay away from various forms of worldly entertainment often quote the Bible to support their point of view. So it might be helpful to look at a representative example and examine the scriptural reasoning that is frequently used by such teachers. The following is an excerpt from Dale Kuiper's booklet "The Christian and Entertainment":

> That movie attendance and television viewing are out of bounds for the Christian, are incompatible with the godly walk of those who are called to be saints, is clear beyond any dispute. Is it not true that movies and television exalt that which is base and depraved, and debase that which is exalted and good? Is it not true that watching the entertainment of the world, its sexual presentations, its violence and bloodshed, its blasphemies against the holy God, makes a person guilty of the sin described in Romans 1:32, "Who knowing the judgment of God, that they which commit such things are worthy of death, not only do the same, but have pleasure in them that do them" [KJV]? Psalm 101, which I encourage you to read right now, is a psalm of David, the man after God's own heart. He says, "I will walk within my house with a perfect heart. I will set no wicked thing before mine eyes. I hate the work of them that turn aside; it shall not cleave to me" [vv. 2–3, KJV]. And a little later in the psalm, "I will not know a wicked person." Although he may be tempted, were he alive today, David would not attend movies nor watch television![4]

First of all, it is certainly true that the popular arts are often motivated by wicked intentions and filled with sinful content. That is why Christians need to be careful and discerning, as I will explain later in this chapter. But does either of the passages mentioned by Kuiper demand that we abstain from all such worldly entertainment? Let's take a closer look at the two passages he quotes.

Romans 1:32. Kuiper asks, "Is it not true that watching the entertainment of the world . . . makes a person guilty of the sin described in Romans 1:32?" The answer is no—not necessarily. Notice that the verse says that we are sinning if we *commit* the sins described in the previous verses, or if we "have pleasure in them that do them" (or "give hearty approval to those who practice them," as the NASB says). It is not our watching those things that is wrong, but approving of them. And is it not possible to observe someone's sin without approving of his sin? Certainly it is; God Himself does it all the time! Likewise, I can watch a movie or listen to some music that has wrong ideas in it, or wrong behavior depicted in it, without rejoicing in that evil. In fact, I can honestly say that in most such cases I am appalled by the objectionable content and wish it was not in there! Sometimes I end up hating the sin more when I see or hear it in the modern media—especially when I am reminded of the consequences of that sin.

So if Romans 1:32 proves anything about the issue of godliness in entertainment, it proves that it is primarily a matter of the heart. Whether we mimic the sin of the world, and whether we like it, is the issue according to the apostle Paul.

Psalm 101. Does this passage indicate that David would never watch movies or television if he were alive today? Only a woodenly literal or biased reading of the text would yield such an idea. I know that many Christians have quoted verse 3 ("I will set no wicked thing before mine eyes," KJV) as a reason for avoiding the popular arts, but I am afraid they are quoting it out of context. That statement does not mean that David would never look at anything evil, any more than "I will know no evil" in verse 4 means that he refused to learn about his enemy, or would not talk to an unsaved person. Likewise, when David says in verse 6 that his "eyes shall be upon the faithful of the land," he doesn't mean that he will be literally gazing at them. The expression means he will approve of them, support them, pray for them, etc. In the same way, "I will set no wicked thing before mine eyes" is understood in terms of literary imagery and surrounding context. The rest of the verse says, "I hate the work of those who fall away; it shall not fasten its grip on me." So David is saying that he will not look upon evil *with approval or pleasure*—though his words do provide a warning that pertains to what we allow ourselves to look upon. Charles Spurgeon, in his *Treasury of David*, captures the sense of the verse well:

> *"I will set no wicked thing before mine eyes."* I will neither delight in it, aim at it, nor endure it. If I have wickedness brought before me by others I will turn away from it, I will not gaze upon it with pleasure. The Psalmist is very sweeping in his resolve . . . no wicked thing: not only shall it not dwell in his heart, but not even before his eyes, for what fascinates the eye is very apt to gain admission into the heart, even as Eve's apple first pleased her sight, and then prevailed over her mind and hand.[5]

So Christians are wise to be very careful about what they take in through their eyes, and discerning about the truth and error depicted in movies and television. But to say that we can never observe evil behavior and remain holy ourselves is going beyond what is written in Psalm 101, or any other passage in the Scriptures.

Again, the heart of the matter is the matter of the heart. Remember two of the passages we studied earlier in this book, both of which are related to issues like this, and both of which indicate the ultimate importance of what goes on inside of us:

> One person regards one day above another, another regards every day alike. Each person must be *fully convinced in his own mind.* He who observes the day, observes it for the Lord, and he who eats, does so for the Lord, for he *gives thanks* to God; and he who eats not, for the Lord he does not eat, and *gives thanks to God.* . . . So then each one of us shall give an account of himself to God. (Rom. 14:5–12)

> Therefore do not go on passing judgment before the time, but wait until the Lord comes who will both bring to light the things hidden in the darkness and disclose *the motives of men's hearts;* and then each man's praise will come to him from God. (1 Cor. 4:5)

Kuiper says in his booklet, "Every man will be judged according to his work, and according to his play." That is certainly true, but notice the basis of judgment mentioned in those verses: When it comes to issues not directly addressed in the Scriptures, God will be looking primarily at the reasons and responses of the heart. And since what goes on inside of us is the most important factor in issues like entertainment, we simply cannot make hard-and-fast rules that every Christian must follow. But though the Bible lacks such precepts, it is filled with *principles* that can lead each individual toward greater godliness, and away from the dangers posed by the modern media.

A Biblical Approach to Entertainment

In regard to the choices we make in this area of our lives, each believer must "give an account of himself to God," as Romans 14:12 says. You should not judge others about their choices, unless there is a clear biblical reason for your judgment, but you must also carefully consider what is right and best for you to do. So to help you in that process, and especially to demonstrate how the Bible addresses the matters of the heart, here are some principles that you can apply. These seven "E's of Entertainment" will hopefully make your entertainment choices easier!

Exalt God. First Corinthians 10:31 says that whatever you do, you should do it "all to the glory of God." Jesus said, "You shall worship the Lord your God, and serve Him only" (Matt. 4:10; Luke 4:8). And Romans 14:6 tells us that our actions are acceptable only when we "give thanks to God" (cf. 1 Thess. 5:18). So when you view or listen to some form of the arts, you need to be glorifying, worshipping, and thanking God while you are doing it.

This means that in one way or another your motive must be to please God. It cannot be merely to please yourself, and it certainly cannot be to enjoy ungodly pleasures. This is perhaps why the idea of avoiding all the popular arts is so popular among Christians—because many have not learned how to enjoy them in a way that brings glory to God. In the past they have watched movies, for instance, only because they wanted to pass the time, or experience the thrill of action, romance, or a good laugh. Or the movies have been a time that they were spending apart from God, because they were gaining enjoyment from things that He would not like. So when a preacher or friend asks, "Would you watch that if Jesus were sitting next to you?" (a good question to ask, by the way), they could never honestly say yes, because they've never taken Jesus with them to see a movie! But I have watched many movies with the full awareness that Jesus is indeed with me, and I have communed with Him during the entire movie. I do this by applying the rest of the principles we will discuss.

Exercise biblical discernment. First Thessalonians 5:21 says that we should "examine everything carefully," and Philippians 4:8 says this: "Finally, brethren, whatever is true, whatever is honorable, whatever is right, whatever is pure, whatever is lovely, whatever is of good repute, if there is any excellence and if anything worthy of praise, let your mind dwell on these things."

How can you apply these verses to the entertainment you enjoy? First, you need to know what the Bible says, and you need to evaluate what you see and hear on the basis of what the Bible says. All of it! If you just let the modern media soak into your mind without exercising biblical discernment, your mind will be turned to mush (morally as well as intellectually). So when you watch, read, or listen to anything, Christian or non-Christian, your brain should be in gear, not in neutral. You need to be interacting with the material in that art form in a manner that is illustrated by the phrase "talking back to your TV." Talk back to your music, talk back to your books, talk back to the movie screen—not out loud (though sometimes that might be appropriate!), but in your heart and mind. And when you see or hear something good, make note of the truth that is communicated or illustrated. When you see or hear something bad, make note of how and why it displeases God, and think about why you should not believe or practice it. This way you will be "taking every thought captive to the obedience of Christ" (2 Cor. 10:5), rather than allowing your mind to be captured by the deceptive and destructive ideas of the enemy.

One way that I have applied this principle in my own life is by "re-interpreting" the lyrics of secular music in a biblical fashion. If I enjoy the sound of a certain kind of music, I can thank God for giving those musicians (even unsaved ones) the talent to produce it. But I recognize that the words of the songs are not coming from hearts that love Christ. So I will often intentionally hear or sing those words with a meaning different from their original intention. For instance, songs about love and sex can often be reinterpreted to apply to my relationship with my wife, even though they may have been written about an unmarried couple. Likewise, single people can think of the lyrics as describing a future marriage relationship they would like to enjoy.[6] This is a legitimate application of Philippians 4:8—finding what is good in the things we observe, and disciplining our minds to "dwell on these things." Of course there are some songs that cannot possibly be reinterpreted in a biblical fashion, even by someone extremely creative. Those songs I do not "dwell on" in my mind, nor do I sing them, because I can find nothing good to enjoy in their lyrics.

Expose evil rather than enjoying it. Ephesians 5:10 summarizes the first two principles we have discussed by encouraging us to "try . . . to learn what is pleasing to the Lord." Then verses 11–12 say, "Do not participate in the unfruitful deeds of darkness, but instead even expose them; for it is disgraceful even to speak of the things which are done by them in secret." God hates sin, and we should too. Therefore it is wrong for us to enjoy it in any way. Unfortunately, so much of modern entertainment is designed with that in mind—to make money by appealing to our sinful nature. This is obviously the purpose of most sexual content, and much of the violence—especially when it is motivated by ungodly revenge and uncontrolled rage, or fixates on the gory details. But there are other, more subtle ways in which the popular arts appeal to our sinful nature, such as our covetousness (beautiful stars, rich characters, exotic locations, etc.) and pride (hero worship, humanistic themes, motivations of self-glory, etc.).

A specific danger that is worth mentioning along these lines is the glorification of evil. Sometimes the villain is portrayed in such a way that the audience is drawn into his evil behavior, to the point of vicarious enjoyment. A classic example of this is the movie *Batman*, in which Jack Nicholson's Joker has more fun than anyone else (by far); the audiences seemed to appreciate and remember this psychotic murderer much more than any of the good guys. Another example, and a rather surprising one, is a *Bibleman* episode in which the Scripture-quoting hero is basically boring compared to the villain, who gets to star in his own MTV-like music video. After watching this show, my children could not quote any of the Bible verses, but they were dancing around singing over and over again, "I am the prince of pride, I got an ego ten miles wide!" So whether it is Batman or Bibleman, be careful that you do not "participate in the unfruitful deeds of darkness" by enjoying sin vicariously.[7]

Perhaps the most prevalent problem with today's popular art (and some of yesterday's) is the way it makes light of matters that should be taken seriously. God and religion are played for laughs, and jokes about sex have almost become synonymous with the concept of comedy. But the Bible is very clear that both of those matters are not to be treated as humorous in any way. The third commandment says, "You shall not take the name of the LORD your God in vain," and the hottest hell is reserved for those who mock God (see Ps. 73:8–9, 17–20). Further, it may surprise you to learn that Ephesians 5:4–6 uses similar language in regard to sexuality:

> There must be no filthiness and silly talk, or coarse jesting, which are not fitting, but rather giving of thanks. For this you know with certainty, that no immoral or impure person or covetous man, who is an idolater, has an inheritance in the kingdom of Christ and God.
>
> Let no one deceive you with empty words, for because of these things the wrath of God comes upon the sons of disobedience.

So it is a sin worthy of God's anger and condemnation to be amused by jokes about Him, and it is equally wrong to laugh at any kind of sexual humor. God wants His name to be treated as holy, and marital intimacy to be viewed as sacred, because it was designed as a picture of the relationship between Christ and the church (Eph. 5:31–32). *That sounds legalistic*, you might think, *to say that we can't laugh at jokes about sex!* But remember that legalism is going *beyond* what is written, and this is something that is clearly written in the pages of Scripture. Such things we must obey and teach, even if they contradict the culture around us, or fly in the face of our own accepted practice.

First John 2:15–16 says, "Do not love the world nor the things in the world. If anyone loves the world, the love of the Father is not in him. For all that is in the world, the lust of the flesh and the lust of the eyes and the boastful pride of life, is not from the Father, but is from the world." This passage has often been quoted to support extrabiblical, universal rules of behavior like "don't go to movies" or "don't listen to secular music." Notice, however, that once again the concern in this passage is a concern about the heart. John does not say that we cannot view or listen to anything that comes from worldly artists, but he does say we are not to love the lust and pride that are in them, and are often presented by them. So I can enjoy (and thank God for) the good things about a Shakespeare play, for instance, while making sure that I do not rejoice in any sin that is glorified, or humor that is inappropriate. I can also "expose the evil" by explaining to my British literature students how and why it is wrong. And to use another example of classic British literature, I can split my sides with my friends and older children as we enjoy the unique and insightful humor in *Monty Python and the Holy Grail*, while skipping scenes like the "virgins in the castle" and the cartoon depicting God. I can expose those examples of inappropriate humor by explaining to my family and others why those parts are wrong, and in doing so we can enjoy a spiritual benefit, as well as a good laugh. We should not watch movies like that too often, however, because of the next principle.

Economize your time. Ephesians 5:15–16 says, "Be careful how you walk, not as unwise men, but as wise, making the most of your time, because the days are evil." Although it may not be sinful for you to watch TV, it certainly would not be wise for you to watch too much of it! And that applies to any form of entertainment. The modern media are so enthralling and effective at capturing your attention and affection, that you must be "careful how you walk," lest entertainment becomes more important and time-consuming than the things that really matter. Movies, TV, and music dominate the lives of so many people today, including Christians, that they do not even have time to *think about* anything spiritual, let alone to serve and worship God. Add to those things net-surfing, computer games, sports, and other hobbies, and we have a society so saturated in entertainment that we are drowning in it! Our souls are so constantly submerged in a sea of pleasure-seeking that we rarely break the surface to contribute anything useful to the Lord or others.

Satan wants you to waste your time, and he is busy producing various forms of entertainment to help you do just that. This is one way that "the days are evil," and one reason why you must plan and work hard to "make the most of your time." That means, first of all, that you should set strict limits on the amount of time and money you spend on entertainment. That part of your life should be only a footnote, whereas the main page should be filled with hard work, studying the Scriptures, worshipping God, and loving and serving others. So often those really important things are the footnote, and our pursuit of pleasure is what preoccupies the mind, consumes the energies of the body, and drains the checkbook. And so we epitomize the godlessness of the last days, becoming "lovers of pleasure rather than lovers of God" (2 Tim. 3:4).

Another application of this principle, however, is that when we do enjoy various forms of entertainment, we should seek to find some redemptive value in them. When we are told to make the most of our time, that includes the time we spend having fun. So ask yourself, "How can this leisure time be spiritually profitable in some way?" One way is to research and find the kind of movies, music, and books that have something interesting and insightful to say about the world that God has made, or even about God Himself. What you observe in that kind of art can make you a better person (when you take Jesus with you), and can also help you build bridges to unbelievers, so that you can share the gospel with them. So before you spend two hours watching a movie, or an hour listening to a CD, I challenge you to consider whether it will have any redemptive value. Will you learn something, be inspired in any way to be a better person, or otherwise be able to *thank God* for those hours (Rom. 14 again)? If not, why waste that time, when it could be used in a way that is much more profitable?[8]

If a fun activity has no redemptive value in itself, then you should find ways to make it more profitable. An example of this would be a day my sons and I spent recently at an amusement park—something we don't do very often, but we got the tickets for that day at a significant discount. So to make the most of our time, we invited another man and his son, who needed some encouragement and discipleship in the faith. We spent the day growing our friendship with these two brothers, and also talking about spiritual issues when the opportunity arose. So the day was not just about having fun, although we did do that, but it was also about fulfilling the Great Commission by making disciples.[9] Now this is not to say that it would have been wrong for me to go alone with my sons that day—I could have thanked God for the friendship I was building with them. But how much more profitable it was for us to have another clearly spiritual purpose for the day, which we could pray about before and after our trip.

Edify your brothers and sisters. This principle can be stated positively, with the example I just mentioned providing an illustration. When we consider how we will have fun or be entertained, we should ask ourselves how we can build up others through it, because the Bible says, "Let all things be done for edification" (1 Cor. 14:26; cf. Rom. 15:2). But the principle can be stated negatively as well, in the sense that we should never do anything that causes a brother or sister to sin (Rom. 14:13; 1 Cor. 8:13). This is especially important in regard to the issue of entertainment, because it is such a matter of the heart, and different hearts respond in different ways to what they see and hear. For example, you may be able to listen to a certain type of music with a clear conscience, but someone else might experience flashbacks to his sinful past when he hears that music, and be tempted to sin. So if you crank that music up while he is riding in your car, you could become a stumbling block to your brother.

In Luke 17:1–2 Jesus says, "It is inevitable that stumbling blocks come, but woe to him through whom they come! It would be better for him if a millstone were hung around his neck and he were thrown into the sea, than that he would cause one of these little ones to stumble." The term "little ones" includes all believers, but it has special reference to children, who can be so easily influenced by the schemes of Satan. And as someone once said, "Where we walk, our children will run." If you love the world too much, your children will probably love it with an unholy passion. If you expose them to too much evil before they have developed sufficient skills of discernment, they will fall under its spell and be spiritually ruined. So be careful that you do not hurt your brothers or sisters, especially the little ones, by the entertainment choices you make.

Excise anything that tempts you to sin. Not only do you need to make sure that you do not tempt others to sin, but you need to excise or cut out any kind of entertainment that will tempt you to sin. This surgical language comes from the words of Jesus in Matthew 5:29–30:

> If your right eye makes you stumble, tear it out and throw it from you; for it is better for you to lose one of the parts of your body, than for your whole body to be thrown into hell. If your right hand makes you stumble, cut it off and throw it from you; for it is better for you to lose one of the parts of your body, than for your whole body to go into hell.

This counsel has been called the principle of radical amputation, because Jesus is clearly saying that we must sometimes take radical and even painful steps if we want to stop sinning. In the figurative picture painted by Christ, the excising of the eye and hand will lessen the ability and opportunity to sin, and will serve as a reminder of its consequences, which will make the offender think twice before sinning again. Likewise, we must make it harder for ourselves to sin, by eliminating opportunities and temptations that we know will lead us astray.[10]

The application of this principle to your entertainment choices should be fairly obvious: If something that you watch, read, or listen to influences you toward evil in your heart or actions, stay far away from it. If you find yourself consumed with a particular hobby, to the point that it has become more important than God, get it out of your life until such a time that you can enjoy it in moderation and propriety. It is indeed legalistic to say that no Christian should ever enjoy worldly forms of entertainment, as we have pointed out, but it is also reasonable to assume that some Christians *should* avoid all or most of them at certain times in their lives. This is often the case with young believers, because they have not yet developed the knowledge of Scripture and the skills of discernment necessary to take in most modern entertainment without being negatively influenced by it. Even though I believe that the *teaching* of my college was legalistic regarding this issue, in a way I am grateful for the strict rules of the school (no TV, movies, etc.), because they forced me to step away from the modern media for a while, to learn the Word of God, and to look at the whole field of entertainment with a more perceptive and critical eye.[11]

Romans 13:12–14 says, "The night is almost gone, and the day is near. Therefore let us lay aside the deeds of darkness and put on the armor of light. Let us behave properly as in the day, not in carousing and drunkenness, not in sexual promiscuity and sensuality, not in strife and jealousy. But put on the Lord Jesus Christ, and *make no provision for the flesh* in regard to its lusts." "Make no provision" comes from a Greek verb that was used, in military parlance, for supplying the front lines in battle. An army cannot fight and win without provisions, and our flesh cannot prevail against the Spirit unless it has material to work with. So we need to cut off the supply lines to our flesh by avoiding any kind of entertainment that tempts us to sin. And if you don't know for sure whether something is spiritually dangerous to you, then apply the seventh and final principle.

Eliminate anything you're not sure about. Romans 14:23 says, "He who doubts is condemned if he eats, because his eating is not from faith; and whatever is not from faith is sin." We discussed this principle of conscience at length in chapter 8 (see pp. 126–29), so we will not linger on it here. But it is important to remember that this principle applies to your entertainment choices as well as all other areas of your life. If you are wondering whether God wants you to watch that movie, listen to that music, read that book, or whatever choice you face, it is better to be safe than sorry. Don't let an insignificant form of entertainment get in the way of the most significant relationship you will ever have! Keep your conscience clean, and take an important step toward a life that is free from guilt.

Entertainment and the Gospel

Your journey toward freedom from guilt does not end with a clean conscience, however. It has to progress farther to the gospel of forgiveness, because in the area of entertainment, as in all areas of our lives, we "all have sinned and fall short of the glory of God" (Rom. 3:23).

Hopefully this extended case study has helped you to see why legalistic rules are not the answer to complex issues like entertainment. But you should have also seen that true biblical holiness requires a great deal of personal work and commitment on your part. Applying the principles we have discussed to entertainment or any other issue in life is difficult to do consistently, and impossible to do perfectly. In fact, it is actually much easier to live by a set of man-made traditions than it is to live in a way that brings glory to God in our "innermost being" (Ps. 51:6). So when we focus on the heart of the matter, as we have in this chapter, we realize how little righteousness we have in ourselves, in contrast to the smug sense of self-righteousness that so often characterizes the legalist. But that is the only path to freedom from all guilt—humbling ourselves before God and receiving the righteousness of Christ through faith in Him.

> For what does the Scripture say? "Abraham believed God, and it was credited to him as righteousness." Now to the one who works, his wage is not credited as a favor, but as what is due. But to the one who does not work, but believes in Him who justifies the ungodly, his faith is credited as

righteousness, just as David also speaks of the blessing on the man to whom God credits righteousness apart from works: "Blessed are those whose lawless deeds have been forgiven, And whose sins have been covered. Blessed is the man whose sin the Lord will not take into account." (Rom. 4:3–8)

Questions for Discussion and Application

1. How would you answer someone who says that Christians should not listen to music or watch movies that are produced by unbelievers?
2. Review the "E's of Entertainment" in this chapter. Have you been practicing them in your own life? If not, how can you start?
3. What do you think about this statement: "Entertainment is one of the most popular gods worshipped by unbelievers today, and many Christians are participating in this idolatry."

Case Study 2: Public Education

A nother controversial issue among Christians, especially today, is the issue of public schools (or government schools, as they are called by their strongest critics). Is it a sin for Christian parents to send their children to these schools? Are home schooling and Christian schools the only legitimate options for believers? Some think so, and in this chapter we will examine some of the reasons for their teaching. I say "we" very intentionally, because I hope that you will read the examples for yourself, and apply what you have learned in this book to evaluating them. So before you go on to read my comments about the first example, for instance, decide what you think is legalistic about it, and what you think is not. Then evaluate my comments, to see whether you agree with me. Hopefully you will find this to be a profitable exercise in biblical discernment.

The C.R.E. Christian Education Memorial

The following position statement was drafted and passed as a motion at the 3rd Presbytery Meeting of the Confederation of Reformed Evangelicals (C.R.E.) in

1999. (I have numbered the paragraphs for the purpose of reference.)

1. All things are to be considered and conducted under the Lordship of Jesus Christ, including education, and especially the education of our covenant children.
2. God has neither charged nor authorized the state to educate children within its civil jurisdiction. God has commanded parents to bring up their children in the education and admonition of the Lord (Eph. 6:4; Deut. 6:7). Given the importance and enormity of the task (Ps. 127:3–5; Deut. 6:7–9), and the impossibility of neutrality in education (Prov. 1:7; Matt. 12:30; Luke 6:40; Col. 2:1–10; 2 Cor. 10:3–5), we do heartily affirm the necessity of educating our children in a manner that is explicitly Christian in content and rigor.
3. Government schools are, by decree and design, explicitly godless, and therefore cannot be considered a legitimate means of inculcating true faith, holy living and a decidedly Christian worldview in the children of Christian parents.
4. Parents who do not fully understand the indispensability of Christian education should be warmly received into membership. However, the leaders of Christ's church must thoroughly understand and plainly teach the divine imperative to disciple our children, the divine prohibition of rendering unto Caesar those who bear God's image (Matt. 22:20–21), the divine warning to those who cause their little ones to stumble (Matt. 18:6) and the divine promises to those who raise their children in faith (Deut.

7:9; Ps. 102:28; Ps. 103:17–18; Prov. 22:6; Luke 1:48–50; Acts 2:39).[1]

In my opinion, this Memorial contains a lot of truth, but also contains some highly questionable interpretation and application of Scripture, which are examples of how the Bible can be sometimes stretched and twisted to support an extrabiblical standard. I believe this statement is legalistic because it goes "beyond what is written" by implying that public schools are not an option for believing parents. Although the statement never says (in so many words), "It is a sin to send your children to a public school," that is basically what it communicates. And some of its framers have communicated that elsewhere, both orally and in print. Therefore it seems to me that they are creating a universal moral standard not actually taught in the Bible. At the very least, their teaching lacks the degree of qualification necessary to keep their adherents from becoming legalistic on this issue.

Now before I go on to explain the reasons for my evaluation, let me say first that all my children are educated by a combination of home school and part-time Christian school. I have never sent my children to a public school, and I do not intend to do so in the future, unless my circumstances or personal preferences change rather drastically. So I have no personal reason to object to this statement, or to any others like it. Also, I admire and appreciate Douglas Wilson, a pastor and author who was one of the framers of this statement and has written several books from the same perspective.[2] God has used Wilson's teaching in my life, through his books *Reforming Marriage* (one of my favorite books on the topic), *Her Hand in Marriage* (a great discussion of biblical courtship), and *To a Thousand Generations*, which was very influential and helpful in my personal theological journey. So I have no personal reason to take exception to his teaching on education, much of which I also agree with. But I do believe he and his fellow elders go too far at times in regard to this particular issue.

Examining the Arguments

Paragraph 1 of the C.R.E. statement is not debatable—we must indeed make our education choices under the lordship of Jesus Christ. But portions of paragraph 2 deserve further examination. Two times it mentions Deuteronomy 6:4–9, which says:

> Hear, O Israel! The LORD is our God, the LORD is one! You shall love the LORD your God with all your heart and with all your soul and with all your might. These words, which I am commanding you today, shall be on your heart. You shall teach them diligently to your sons and shall talk of them when you sit in your house and when you walk by the way and when you lie down and when you rise up. You shall bind them as a sign on your hand and they shall be as frontals on your forehead. You shall write them on the doorposts of your house and on your gates.

This passage definitely teaches what the C.R.E. elders say, that "God has commanded parents to bring up their children in the education and admonition of the Lord." But it is used by many advocates of Christian education to prove much more than that. Because this passage is so often quoted in the context of this issue, it is important to take a closer look at how it relates to education.

Deuteronomy 6, more than any other passage, is quoted by Christian-school advocates to argue that it is wrong for children to be sent to a public school. It also happens to be the passage most quoted by home-school advocates to argue that it is wrong for children to be sent to a Christian school (the passage says parents must teach their children, not schoolteachers). Both cannot be right, so is it not possible that both are wrong? I think so, and I think that where both go wrong is by going beyond what is actually written in these words of Moses.

Douglas Wilson, for example, says in his book *Standing on the Promises* that "Christian parents are morally obligated to keep their children out of government schools," and he quotes Deuteronomy 6 as support. He explains the passage in this way: "All of life is under the authority of God's revealed Word, and children were to be taught in terms of this comprehensive authority *all the time*. . . . A thorough and biblical instruction can only be provided successfully if it is happening *all the time*."[3] The problem is that "all the time" is a sloppy, if not completely incorrect, rephrasing of the words of Moses. Can we really be teaching our children the Bible at every single moment of the day? Of course not. So it would be more accurate to say that God wants us to teach them "at various times," "in many different circumstances of life," or "in the milieu of life," as some have put it.

The way in which particular parents choose to do that, however, is an individual matter between the parents and God. A "home school only" advocate would say that I am not obeying this passage because my children go to school two days a week, where they are not taught by their parents. But I would say that I *am* permeating their lives with Scripture, though I choose to make use of others to help me in that process. Likewise, a public-school parent could say that he is teaching the Bible diligently to his children when he is with them, at home and in church, but allows knowledgeable people to help with the other subjects. He also can talk to his children about God's perspective on the subjects they study in school, and he can do this when they sit in their house, when they walk by the way, when they lie down, and when they rise up. Even public-school parents are with their children at those times, so there is no necessary reason why they cannot obey what this passage says. It may be more difficult, but it is not impossible with God's help, as many godly public-school parents have demonstrated.

The "Myth of Neutrality" Issue

Paragraph 2 also contains a reference to "the impossibility of neutrality in education." This is another foundational reason for the belief that public schools are necessarily harmful to children. Douglas Wilson explains this idea at length in all his books about education, but here is a representative example, from *Excused Absence: Should Christian Kids Leave Public Schools?*

> Education is one of the most religious things we do. Consequently, any pretense of religious neutrality in the process of educating children in some plain-vanilla fashion is a myth that will lead to enormous confusion. The myth distorts the nature of knowledge, which is the last thing an educator should do.
>
> As we reject the myth of neutrality, we must remember that we are not rejecting neutrality as a bad thing, but rather as an *impossible* thing. The problem with the government schools is that they cannot be neutral, even if the people running them try their level best. Government schools cannot be neutral any more than they can fly to the moon or walk on water.[4]

The discussion about the "myth of neutrality" is a very important one, and I think that every Christian parent should read Wilson's comments on the matter, and consider them carefully. He is right, for instance, that by not mentioning God, public school teachers are actually saying something about God—that He is not very important! Any parents who consider sending their children to public schools should be aware of this problem. But unfortunately, Wilson lays too much of a load on the shoulders of what may be his best contribution to the issue. If he simply taught this principle and challenged parents to consider it carefully, he would not be going "beyond what is written." But he uses it to support the contention that Christian kids should "leave public schools" (the subtitle of the book). The fact is, however, that the "myth of neutrality" simply cannot bear the burden of proof for such a dogmatic and universal statement. What if the parents do understand this dynamic, and train their children at home to think about God while they are at school? What if the children themselves have a heart of worship while they go about their day there? Even if Christ is not in the school itself, Christians can take Him there with them.

The same "myth of neutrality" argument could be used to say that a Christian should not work for a secular company, because business is "one of the most religious things we do" (Eph. 6:5–8; Col. 3:22–25). And along with almost every other argument against public-school attendance, it could also be used to argue that college-age Christians should never spend four years at a secular university— something that many "no public school" parents allow their children to do. Or in regard to younger children again, we could say that they should not spend so many hours practicing and playing in a community sports league, especially under a non-Christian coach. We could say it is *impossible* to coach sports in a neutral way, no matter how hard someone tries!

But the fact is that, although the overall philosophy of education can never be neutral, parts of it can be. For instance, there may conceivably be an hour in a public-school math class that looks exactly like an hour in a Christian-school math class. The teacher says the same things, the math problems are the same—the only difference may be what goes on before or after that hour (prayer to start the class, discussions about spiritual issues after class, etc.). It is not sinful, nor is it necessarily bad education, for there to be an hour of math class where God is not mentioned. Is not that hour morally neutral in itself? What will make it good or evil for each person is not the content of the class, but the heart of the person while in it. Certainly all reasonable people would have to admit this is the case—but once we admit that some degree of neutrality does exist in education, the "myth of neutrality" argument no longer can be used as support for a universal moral standard. Since what really matters is what goes on before or after the neutral instruction, and what goes on in the heart of the student, you can see why some parents might say that they prefer to take advantage of the book learning in a public school, while they train their children at home to love and worship God in all they do, and wherever they go. And perhaps you can agree that many children, especially those with godly parents, have attended public schools and walked with the Lord during and after their time there.

The C.R.E. statement includes some proof texts to support "the impossibility of neutrality in education," but unfortunately they do not prove anything. They all refer, in one way or another, to the influence that both good teaching and bad teaching can have on people, but they do not address whether or not some parts of education can be neutral. The one possible exception is Matthew 12:30, where Jesus says, "He who is not with Me is against Me." But this is a classic example of arbitrary proof-texting, because Jesus also said in Mark 9:40, "He who is not against us is for us." A public-school advocate could quote that verse in support of his "neutral" educators! Context is the key to understanding these two passages, of course, and in the context of Matthew 12:30 Jesus is clearly speaking about the kind of teaching that is overtly antagonistic to Him (cf. vv. 31–32).

Paragraph 2 also mentions "the necessity of educating our children in a manner that is explicitly Christian in content and rigor." This is rather unclear and raises enough questions to limit its relevance. How explicitly Christian does education need to be? Do math class, lunch break, and P.E. need to be filled with Bible instruction? If not, and we say that children can be instructed in the Bible at other times, why couldn't some parents decide to do that at home and church, rather than in school? I think that all devoted Christians would agree with this statement, but there are different ways to make an education "explicitly Christian." The statement itself does not demand that we choose a particular type of school.

Paragraph 3 makes me wonder if the framers of the statement really understand those who differ with them. I say that because no one thinks that public schools are a "legitimate means of inculcating true faith, holy living and a decidedly Christian worldview." My Christian friends who have their kids in a public school would say that the home and the church are the places where those things happen. So again, this paragraph does not prove the point that the Memorial is trying to make.

Effects on the Church

Paragraph 4 begins with this sentence, "Parents who do not fully understand the indispensability of Christian education [presumably those who have their children in a public school] should be warmly received into membership." This first part seems to be an admirable attempt to avoid an extreme approach to this issue, and perhaps even to avoid the problem of legalism. But then the statement goes on to say that the leaders of the church should teach that what those parents are doing is wrong (at least in most cases). What if these people do not agree with this teaching and do not remove their children from the public school? Will they then be removed from the church? Matthew 18:15–17 would seem to require that, if indeed what they are doing is a sin. But an even more fundamental question is this: Will public-school parents and children want to stay in a church that says they are living in sin? And will any public-school parents and children want anything to do with such a church in the first place, when it is known throughout the community that this is what the church teaches?

This is an example of how legalism, even in subtle forms, can become inimical to the mission and message of the church of Jesus Christ. The *mission* of the church is to reach people like public-school parents and children for Christ, but this legalistic perspective builds walls rather than bridges between the church and people like that. It would be better to say something like this to parents: "We do not condemn any particular educational option as wrong in itself; this choice is between you and God. But we want to help educate you about education from the Scriptures, so you can make the best choice for your family." That approach would make public-school parents and children comfortable enough to come to the church, build helpful relationships there, and work through these issues with the support and acceptance of the body. But saying or implying that their education choice is necessarily sinful makes it highly unlikely that such people will attend and be assimilated into the church. So the church will likely have very few members, if any, who have their children in a public school. Does that reflect the diverse nature of the body of Christ described in 1 Corinthians 12?

I am also concerned that the *message* of the church may be endangered by legalism in regard to education. If the leaders say that public schools are wrong, and all the children in the church are in home or Christian schools, then I fear the impression will be given that if you want to be a Christian, you must have your children in a home school or Christian school. So a person considering the Christian faith might think, "If I become a Christian, I will have to take on this huge task of homeschooling, which I know nothing about, or somehow make enough money to pay for Christian school." That may seem daunting enough to end all consideration! Jesus did tell people to "calculate the cost" of following Him (Luke 14:25–35), but we need to be careful not to "add to the cost" a rule that is not actually taught by the Scriptures. That was the concern of the Jerusalem council when they determined to "lay no greater burden" upon the Gentiles who were coming to Christ (Acts 15:28–29).[5]

Children and Caesar

Paragraph 4 of the Christian Education Memorial concludes with a series of biblical principles that seem to be intended as more support for the idea that public schools are not an option for believers. But again, do they really prove that assertion? Regarding the first one, all committed believers, even those who are public-school parents, believe in "the divine imperative to disciple our children." Parents differ, however, on exactly how God wants them to do that in regard to education choices.

The second principle mentioned is "the divine prohibition of rendering unto Caesar those who bear God's image (Matt. 22:20–21)." This is an unfortunate example of stretching Scripture and taking it out of context to support what you want to say, even though the Scripture itself is not talking about what you are talking about. The whole context of Jesus' words in Matthew 22:15–22 is about money—there is no reason to think that He had children and education on His mind at all. Also, Jesus never actually says, "Do not render unto Caesar what belongs to God." Yet Douglas Wilson calls this an "important implication" and uses it as proof for his teaching about public schools. Notice his reasoning in this excerpt from *Excused Absence*: "We not only should render to Caesar what is Caesar's, but we also must not render to Caesar what is God's. What should we use to determine 'what is God's image' in this context? Who bears God's image—the *imago Dei*? The answer certainly includes our children. This means that our children may not be rendered to Caesar."[6]

This progression of thought seems cogent at first glance, but upon further examination is full of holes. The first one, which I already suggested, is that Wilson makes a possible implication of Jesus into a command of Jesus. The second is that "the things that are God's" in Matthew 22:21 refers not to people, but to the things people possess. What the context really indicates is that Jesus is most likely referring to our tithes and offerings to the church, as opposed to the taxes we pay to the government. And finally, it seems that Wilson's argument proves too much. If I say children bear God's image and should therefore not be in government schools, I could on the same grounds say that adults, who also bear God's image, should not work for the government, attend government colleges, or serve in the military. We must be careful about turning possible implications into dogmatic commands, and making inferences that land us well beyond what is written.

In *Excused Absence*, Wilson continues his argument by citing Samuel's warning to the people of Israel that their children would be used by the king to further his agenda (1 Sam. 8, which also says the same thing about their crops, their slaves, and the adults themselves). He says, "In a similar way, by sending our kids to government schools, we are giving them to 'Caesar' as slaves to our cultural godlessness." Then he concludes, "When we take the Deuteronomy 6 [teach your children the law of God] and 1 Samuel 8 passages together, the conclusion is inescapable: *Christian parents who send Christian children to government schools when those children are uneducated and unprepared are rendering to Caesar what is God's.*"[7]

That conclusion is inescapable? Saying so doesn't make it so! Wilson is clearly saying that public-school parents are sinning against God, but all he actually proves is that they are disobeying two questionable inferences from the Old Testament and a command he attributes to Matthew 22:21, which is not actually in the verse!

Paragraph 4 of the C.R.E. statement closes with a reference to "the divine warning to those who cause their little ones to stumble (Matt. 18:6) and the divine promises to those who raise their children in faith." Presumably these items are also considered to be support for why it is wrong to send children to public school. But if that is the case, they would both be examples of a logical fallacy called *petitio principii* ("begging the question" or "circular reasoning"), because they already assume what must be proven.[8] It is not necessarily true that public-school parents are causing their little ones to stumble, or failing to raise their children in faith. What has not been proven cannot be cited as proof.

As I conclude my thoughts on the teaching of the C.R.E. and Douglas Wilson, please remember that I do believe the issues they raise about education are very important for Christian parents to consider carefully. My own careful consideration of them has led me to choose home and Christian school, and I have been helped in that process by Wilson's writings in particular. What I also believe, however, is that it is a form of legalism to say or imply that it is a sin to have children in a public school. That is simply going too far. Or to put it in scriptural terms, it is going beyond what is written. And I do think that the C.R.E. and Douglas Wilson have done that in this case, though I also believe that they have struggled with the issue of legalism and even made some attempts to avoid it.[9]

I cannot thoroughly examine all the arguments about public education in this brief discussion, nor is that my purpose here; so I am sure there are major omissions in my treatment of the topic. But I humbly submit that a better approach to this issue would be to say that there is no education option that is necessarily wrong in itself, and then to talk about the biblical principles that apply, and the pros and cons of each option. Then let parents decide for themselves and stand before God on their own. To put it again in biblical terms, we should be fully convinced in our own mind about what we choose for ourselves (Rom. 14:5), and careful not to judge the choices of our brothers (Rom. 14:13).

A Modest Proposal

Now that we have discussed this particular topic at length, I would like to make use of it to provide an illustration that applies to all other forms of legalism as well. I want you to see how a certain type of reasoning, which goes beyond the Scriptures by stretching and twisting them, can seem to prove almost any nonbiblical moral standard. So I would like to make a case for why it is a moral necessity that Christian parents take their children out of secular community soccer leagues.

There is no Bible verse that says, "Don't put your children in local soccer leagues," but many biblical principles make it very clear that this is not an option for believers. Though I could provide more, let me just mention six reasons for the indispensability of having your children play soccer only at home, or in explicitly Christian leagues.

1. The Bible says that we must love God with all our mind, heart, soul, and strength (Matt. 22:37; Mark 12:30; Luke 10:27). We must do this at all times in life, including when we play sports like soccer. We must think and act like Christians when we play soccer, because all of life is to be lived under the lordship of Jesus Christ (1 Cor. 10:31; 2 Cor. 5:9).
2. Community soccer leagues are normally planned and organized by unbelievers, and most of the coaches are unbelievers. So the way the league is structured and all the instruction that our children will receive from such people are godless and contrary to the Word of God (Ps. 1:1–2; 1 Cor. 2:14; 2 Cor. 6:14–17). Even if a Christian adult happens to be involved in the league, its secular nature prevents him or her from teaching about sports or

coaching the team in an explicitly Christian manner. That is not acceptable according to the principles in number 1 above—our goal should be nothing less than an explicitly Christian soccer league, for our God demands no less.

3. There is no such thing as neutrality when it comes to the instruction and direction that take place in the training and coaching of team sports. Either they are done for God, or they are against God (Prov. 1:7; Matt. 12:30; Luke 6:40; Col. 2:1–10; 2 Cor. 10:3–5). And since God will be left out of the planning and conducting of a community soccer league, the many hours our children spend in practice and games without Him as the center of this activity will be teaching them that He is not important in this significant area of their lives.

4. Most soccer leagues today are, of course, run by a city Parks and Recreation Department or some other arm of local government. Such government soccer leagues are, by decree and design, explicitly godless, and therefore cannot be considered a legitimate means of inculcating true faith, holy living, and a decidedly Christian worldview in the children of Christian parents. In fact, Christian parents who enroll their children in such programs are disregarding the teaching of Christ by "rendering unto Caesar the things that are God's" (cf. Matt. 22:21). These children bear God's image, but their parents are allowing them to be under the authority and influence of a pagan system for a significant amount of time each week.

5. Allowing our children to participate in secular soccer leagues will expose them to all kinds of evil that they are not yet capable of discerning and resist-

ing. Hence we will be causing these little ones to stumble (Matt. 18:6). At the games and practices, there will be displays of anger, bad sportsmanship of various kinds, parents yelling at the referees, immodestly dressed women, unhealthy snacks, and worst of all, the company of other children who are from unbelieving and semi-Christian homes. Our children may even develop friendships with some of these ungodly children, and want to spend even more time with them outside of soccer. Remember, "the companion of fools will suffer harm" (Prov. 13:20).

6. Finally, Christian parents who keep their kids in secular soccer leagues are keeping this pagan system in existence, and in that way are participating in the evil that goes on. I am convinced that if all Christian parents would pull out of their community soccer leagues, the entire system would collapse in less than a year. Then the Christian leagues we start, in addition to the books and conferences on how to conduct them, would enjoy astronomical success!

Can you see how this case I have made goes beyond what is written, even though it may seem pious and biblical, and may be motivated by a sincere desire to please the Lord? You may say my soccer arguments go way too far, but hopefully you can see how those who use the same arguments about public schools, and other extrabiblical issues, are going at least a little too far. And remember that to whatever degree we go beyond what is written, we are susceptible to all the dangers of judging and legalism that have been discussed in this book.

Southern Baptist Statements

In the summer of 2004 the Southern Baptist Convention held its annual meeting in Indianapolis, Indiana. As always, numerous resolutions were proposed to the Convention by churches, concerned groups, and individual members within the denomination. One of them concerned Christian education and was controversial enough to generate quite a bit of press. It was voted down by the Convention, perhaps because it is another illustration of a statement that has many good qualities, but unfortunately goes beyond what is written.

The resolution, submitted by T. C. Pinckney and Bruce Shortt, presents the same basic ideas that are mentioned in the C.R.E. Memorial, before concluding in this way:

> Now, therefore, be it resolved that the 2004 Annual Meeting of the Southern Baptist Convention encourages all officers and members of the Southern Baptist Convention and the churches associated with it to remove their children from the government schools and see to it that they receive a thoroughly Christian education. . . .
>
> Be it further resolved that the 2004 Annual Meeting of the Southern Baptist Convention encourages all churches . . . to work energetically to counsel parents regarding their obligation to provide their children with a Christian education.[10]

At first this proposal may seem to avoid legalism, because the first paragraph above merely "encourages" people to take their children out of public schools. But the second paragraph says that Christian education is an "obligation"—and the rest of the resolution makes clear that the authors do not consider public schools to be a form of

Christian education. So this statement also goes too far by implying that public-school parents are sinning.

But there was another resolution submitted to the Southern Baptist Convention in 2004 that did not get any press coverage. It also was not adopted by the Convention, for whatever reason, but I think it is an excellent example of a position statement that challenges people to think about this very important issue, while carefully avoiding the problem of legalism. It was written by Phil Kell of the California Baptist Foundation:

> **Whereas** the Southern Baptist Council on Family Life reported to the 2002 Annual Meeting of the Southern Baptist Convention that 88 percent of the children raised in evangelical homes leave church at the age of 18 never to return; and
>
> **Whereas** we have no greater priority as Christian parents and grandparents than raising the next Godly generation of Christian disciples; and
>
> **Whereas** the Scriptures clearly teach that parents are primarily responsible for the protection, education and training of children, and fathers are clearly admonished to bring children up in the nurture and admonition of the Lord (Eph. 6:4); and
>
> **Whereas** our churches are committed to assisting parents with the task of raising Christian disciples who have not been taken captive through hollow and deceptive philosophy, which depends on human tradition and the basic principles of this world rather than on Christ (Col. 2:8); and
>
> **Whereas** the public schools and the humanistic environment permitted therein teach our children, among other things, to accept: evolution as factual science, sexual immorality as personal diversity, abortion as an accept-

able choice, all religions as moral equivalents, the Bible as just another book, prayer as unconstitutional speech, vulgarity and promiscuity as social norms, and greed as the American way; and

Whereas in the public schools our children and grandchildren are becoming increasingly subject to violence, drugs, unhealthy lifestyles, gang activity, worldly peer pressure and a Godless worldview; and

Whereas we believe Christians should be encouraged to be salt and light as they serve as teachers and administrators in the increasingly hostile and difficult environment of public education, and we commend those of our number who have served and are serving sacrificially in these most important roles; and

Whereas we recognize that while some of our children and grandchildren are able to influence their peers for the cause of Christ, countless others are irreparably damaged and permanently lost to the cause of Christ by the worldly teaching and secular influences encountered on public school campuses; and

Whereas we question the ability of innocent children to withstand the increasingly worldly influences of the public schools and believe the loss of many of our children [from] the cause of Christ may be due, in part, to these influences; now therefore, be it

Resolved that the messengers to the 2004 Annual Meeting of the Southern Baptist Convention strongly encourage the churches of the SBC during the next year to honestly and prayerfully investigate and evaluate the effect that the public schools are having on the children and grandchildren in their congregations; and be it further

Resolved that our churches be encouraged to honestly and prayerfully investigate and evaluate whether other educational alternatives such as serious Christian schools and

Christian home schooling are doing a better job of assisting parents and grandparents with the task of raising children and grandchildren who are true disciples of Christ; and be it further

Resolved that our churches be encouraged to honestly and prayerfully investigate and evaluate how the church can better assist parents and grandparents with the task of training and educating the children and grandchildren in their congregation to be true disciples of Christ; and be it further

Resolved that after a year of prayer, investigation, study and honest evaluation by our churches the messengers to the 2005 Annual Meeting of this body present such resolutions or motions as may be appropriate in light of these efforts, in order to strengthen the work of our churches as they strive to assist parents and grandparents in their God-given assignment of raising children committed to the cause of Christ.[11]

Addressing this second resolution on their website, the authors of the first one say, "We do not believe this resolution goes far enough. The evidence is in—it's time to get our kids out of government schools." This is probably true for many Christian parents, but we simply cannot prove from Scripture that all Christian parents must do it. So I find the approach of the second resolution to be a good model of how to address an issue like this thoughtfully and thoroughly, but without going beyond what is written. I hope it will be helpful to you as you consider this important issue, and others like it. And I hope we can all resist the temptation to "play the Holy Spirit" in people's lives, by telling them what conclusions they must reach and what applications they must make from the principles in Scripture. If we lovingly and faithfully teach those principles to Christians, and then leave them to the Spirit, He is able to lead them where they need to go. And to do this we must place our trust in divine guidance, rather than in the strength of our own ideas and influence, for the renewal of God's people will occur " 'not by might nor by power, but by My Spirit,' says the LORD of hosts" (Zech. 4:6).

Questions for Discussion and Application

1. Do you agree with the author's assessment of the "Memorial" in this chapter? Why or why not?
2. What would a non-Christian couple likely think if they visited a church and found out that most or all of the families in the church have their children in home school or Christian school? How could that problem be avoided?
3. How could you use the same type of arguments used against public education to make a case against other activities, like eating at a restaurant that has a bar, voting in public elections, and shopping at Barnes & Noble?

Legalism and the Gospel

T his discussion of the gospel, and how it relates to legalism, is not reserved for the conclusion of this book because it is unimportant. On the contrary, what I say here should inform everything I have said previously, because the understanding and application of the gospel is one of the primary solutions to the problems this book has addressed. Also, this conclusion should effectively up the ante and raise the stakes for everything you have read so far, because you will realize that legalism is not merely an error that will hinder your spiritual growth as a Christian—it can also present a danger to your eternal soul!

Those who are legalistic in regard to sanctification are often, to one degree or another, legalistic in regard to salvation as well—whether they realize it or not. This is illustrated in a rather obvious fashion by movements such as Mormonism, the Jehovah's Witnesses, and Roman Catholicism, whose theology of "salvation by faith plus works" is accompanied by all kinds of extrabiblical rules and requirements. But the same dynamic is also evident in evangelical groups where forms of legalism have gained a foothold, and distortions of the gospel have arisen as well.[1] A scriptural example of this can be found in the book of Galatians, where it is sometimes difficult to tell when Paul is talking about legalism in connection with salvation and when he is talking about legalism in connection with sanctification. Apparently both problems existed in those churches.

What is the connection between the two? How are legalism and misrepresentations of the gospel related? Hopefully as we consider this problem, an important solution will also become evident.

First, *a wrong understanding of the gospel leads to legalism.* The idea that works of our own, in addition to faith, are necessary for salvation is what many have called legalism (because obedience to the law is a condition for forgiveness). This is what I refer to as "legalism in justification" in contrast to "legalism in sanctification," which is the adding of rules and traditions to the ethical teaching of the Bible. My point here is that legalism in justification leads to legalism in sanctification. If you believe, to whatever degree, that your salvation is dependent upon your moral performance, you will tend to create or gravitate to moral standards that are "beyond what is written," so you can have more assurance that you are really making the grade, and that God really loves you.

The Pharisees were extreme examples of this dynamic, as we discussed in chapter 7. They feared that God would not accept them if they were not righteous enough, and so they constructed fences to keep from getting anywhere near sin. And as time went on, they began to trust more in their fences than in the grace of God Himself. What they needed to realize, more than anything else, was that none of us can be righteous enough in ourselves (Rom. 3:10), so God freely gives us His righteousness as a gift, through faith in Christ (Rom. 3:21–24).

But the Pharisees were not the only ones who missed the grace of God—evangelical Christians today make the same mistake, though in more subtle ways. Consider the following story and comments from Harry Reeder.

Harry was playing golf with another Christian. They came to a hole where a major highway ran along one side of the fairway. His friend stepped up to hit a drive, and sliced it toward the highway. It was a hard drive, and there was a heavy wind that caught the ball and sent it sailing farther toward the road. Harry was wondering what damage the high-speed projectile would cause when it flew into the sea of cars. But just before the ball could wreak havoc on the freeway, it ricocheted off the top of a tall pine tree, bounced straight down a long stretch of the paved cart path, and came to rest about ten yards in front of the green! Harry looked in disbelief at his friend, who said with a smile, "I had my quiet time this morning."

That comment was tongue-in-cheek, of course, but it illustrates the way Christians often view their relationship with God. Instead of being motivated by the joy of spending time with God and bringing pleasure to Him, we have our quiet time in order to earn brownie points so that our day might go better. And instead of trusting in His grace when things go wrong, knowing that even our trials are a part of His loving sovereign plan, we fear that He has somehow forgotten us or stopped loving us. But we must remember something else that Harry Reeder says:

> God loves us *in Christ*—not because of who we are or what we do, but because of who Christ is and what He has done. So since God will never stop loving Christ, He will never stop loving us! Nor will He ever love us more or less than He does right now—*in Christ*.

Think of someone who is a new Christian, perhaps one who is still struggling with serious problems like alcoholism or drug abuse. Now imagine that this person will go on to conquer his addictions, raise a godly family, become a successful pastor, and win thousands of people to Christ. What you need to remember is that the new, struggling believer will never be more called than he is right now. He will never be more born again than he is right now. He will never be more justified than he is right now. He will never be more adopted as a son of God than he is right now. He will hopefully grow to be more like Christ in his practical living, and he will also grow to enjoy his relationship with God more and more. He also may have to endure less discipline from his loving Father. But his Father cannot love him more than He already does in Christ.[2]

That is the gospel: in ourselves we are more sinful than we ever dare to admit, but in Christ we are more loved and accepted than we ever dare to hope. But when people do not understand that blessed truth of forensic justification or positional righteousness, they seek to find ways to make themselves more acceptable to God, and they go beyond what is written.

Second, the converse is also true: *legalism leads to a wrong understanding of the gospel.* Once we have created universal moral standards outside the clear teaching of the Bible, we now have to answer the question, "What about Christians who do not agree with those standards, or practice them?" And the response often comes, "Well, they are probably not true Christians." For example, if drinking alcohol is a sin, but a professing Christian persists in it even after being told it is wrong, then she must have a stubborn heart of unbelief, and love her liquor more than God. If Christian couples choose to put their children in the government schools, and continue to do so after being taught why that choice is wrong, then are they not breaking covenant with God and casting doubt on their profession of faith? Someone who seems powerless to give up smoking must not have the Holy Spirit inside of him, and so on. Put this together with the fact that legalists tend to focus excessively on their man-made rules, and those rules become so mixed with the gospel that they cannot be distinguished from the gospel.

Faith without works cannot save, and good works are a necessary evidence that our faith is genuine (James 2:14–20), so it is true that a lifestyle of sin calls into question the validity of a person's profession of faith (cf. Matt. 7:21–23; 1 John 3:4–10). But that is true of a lifestyle of disobeying the commands of Scripture, not the traditions and rules of men. And as Paul said in 1 Corinthians 4:6, there is something about going beyond what is written that produces spiritual pride in us. When we obey God's commands by the power of the Holy Spirit, He helps us to remain humble by giving God all the glory for our obedience. But when we obey man-made rules without the power of the Spirit, we tend to take the credit ourselves, and slip into a "works righteousness" mentality.

I have attempted to explain some of the reasons why there is a connection between legalism in regard to sanctification and legalism in regard to salvation. Whether my explanations are helpful or not, there is no question that connection exists. Therefore you should take these final words as a heart-felt warning to avoid all forms of legalism at all costs, so you will not be deceived into believing a false gospel of works-righteousness, or have a false assurance based on your ability to keep man-made moral standards. True assurance of salvation comes from trusting in Christ alone for our righteousness, and from experiencing the fruit of the Spirit, which are primarily inward changes of the heart (Gal. 5:22–23). Outward godliness is sometimes mentioned in Scripture as an evidence for salvation, but more often than not it is inward godliness that serves as the test of faith (Heb. 3:14; 1 John 1:9; 2:9–10; 2:15; 2:24).

Take 2 Corinthians 13:5, for instance: "Test yourselves to see if you are in the faith; examine yourselves! Or do you not recognize this about yourselves, that Jesus Christ is in you—unless indeed you fail the test?" Paul says you can know that you are a true Christian if "Jesus Christ is *in you.*" On the other hand, notice how the legalists in Scripture find their assurance in their external behavior: The false believers who are rejected by Christ at the judgment will say, "Lord, Lord, did we not prophesy in Your name, and in Your name cast out demons, and in Your name perform many miracles?" (Matt. 7:22); the Pharisee at the temple prayed, "God, I thank You that I am not like other people: swindlers, unjust, adulterers, or even like this tax-gatherer. I fast twice a week; I pay tithes of all that I get" (Luke 18:11–12); and the false teachers in Galatia were telling people that being circumcised guaranteed their place in heaven. But to those same people Paul says, "Neither is circumcision anything, nor uncircumcision, but a *new creation*" (Gal. 6:15).

So again I encourage you to use Paul's words in 1 Corinthians 4:6 as a motto for your own life. When it comes to your understanding and communication of the gospel, "Do not go beyond what is written." What is written in the Word of God is a doctrine of salvation by *faith alone*, so never add anything to the free grace of justification through Christ our Savior. "For by grace you have been saved through faith; and that not of yourselves, it is the gift of God; not as a result of works, so that no one may boast" (Eph. 2:8–9). And when it comes to your life as a Christian, "Do not go beyond what is written." Learn what the Word of God says, and how it applies to your life, then practice it with all your might. But never allow ideas of your own, or those of any other human being, to be placed on an equal level with God's divine revelation.

Questions for Discussion and Application

1. What is "the gospel"? Explain it in your own words.
2. How does a wrong understanding of the gospel lead to legalism?
3. How does legalism lead to a wrong understanding of the gospel?
4. How will your life be changed as a result of reading this book? Share the changes with someone else who can pray for you as you seek to follow the Lord in those ways.

The Ultimate Human Judgment

W hile I was writing this book, I had a brief discussion about its contents with a friend. He asked me, "So how can we judge whether someone is a Christian or not?" That is the ultimate human judgment—forming an opinion about whether someone is headed to heaven or to hell! And if that question came to his mind, it will probably occur to many others as well. Perhaps it has occurred to you as you have read this book. So I would like to address it briefly in this appendix.

Judging That Someone Is a Christian

First of all, as disconcerting as it may seem, it is not possible for you to know *with certainty* that anyone else is a true Christian. Second Timothy 2:19 says that "the Lord knows those who are His," and we can know that we ourselves are true believers through the witness of the Holy Spirit (Rom. 8:16) and the evidence of His work in our lives (1 John 5:13). But when it comes to the faith of others, we can never be totally sure that it is real (during this life), because faith is something that exists entirely in the heart of a person, where only God can see completely and accurately (Jer. 17:9–10). Also, numerous Scriptures—and many painful experiences—attest to the fact that people can appear to be true believers in every way, but prove to be false when they turn away from the faith (Heb. 6:4–8; 1 John 2:19) or are rejected by the Lord at the final judgment (Matt. 7:21–23).

So our relationship to other professing Christians as brothers and sisters is based on a *presumption* of faith. Or to put it another way, we *call* them believers, *accept* them as believers, and *treat* them as believers. We should do this without an excessive curiosity or concern about whether their faith is real, leaving that issue largely to God. But we also should encourage one another to persevere in the faith, and at times challenge others to examine themselves regarding the genuineness of their faith. Consider these two passages:

> Take care, brethren, that there not be in any one of you an evil, unbelieving heart that falls away from the living God. But encourage one another day after day, as long as it is still called "Today," so that none of you will be hardened by the deceitfulness of sin. (Heb. 3:12–13)

> Test yourselves to see if you are in the faith; examine yourselves! Or do you not recognize this about yourselves, that Jesus Christ is in you—unless indeed you fail the test? (2 Cor. 13:5)

Notice that the biblical writers referred to their readers as Christians (or brothers, believers, saints, members of the body, etc.). But they also recognized that some of those who were outwardly a part of the church might not be *truly* Christians in their hearts. They knew that there will always be tares among the wheat (Matt. 13:37–43). But regarding who are the wheat and who are the tares, they left that judgment to God—except in the case of those who were under church discipline. The biblical writers did not attempt to determine or distinguish true believers from false believers within the church. They accepted people's profession of faith, as long as it was a credible or biblical profession; and they treated all members of the church as believers, unless the process of church discipline proved otherwise. We should therefore do the same.

A question that is likely to arise at this point is, "It makes sense that we should accept as a brother whoever has a credible profession of faith, but what exactly is a credible profession of faith?" Without going into an extensive discussion of this issue, or even providing all the biblical support for it, I would suggest that a credible profession of faith includes an acceptance of the essential attributes of God as expressed clearly in the Scriptures and in the historic creeds of the faith, such as His eternality, spirituality, sovereignty, and trinity (especially the deity of Christ, which is so often denied by pseudo-Christian cults). A credible profession of faith also includes an affirmation of salvation by grace alone through faith in Christ alone. (When people ask me, "What is a true Christian?" or something similar, my short answer is "Someone who trusts in Christ alone for salvation.") And finally, a credible profession of faith also includes a commitment to and identification with God's people, the church, through baptism and whatever form of membership the church leaders require. If after being taught about the importance of these things, a professing believer refuses to be baptized, or to commit himself to a local body of believers, his profession would lack credibility.[1]

Judging That Someone Is Not a Christian

It is acceptable to conclude that someone who denies the orthodox doctrines of the Trinity, or who claims to be saved by something other than faith in Christ alone, is not a Christian. And it is not sinful judging to think that someone who is clearly unwilling to identify and fellowship with God's people should be treated as an unbeliever. Those judgments are based on what a person *says* or *does*, evaluated by the teaching of Scripture. But I have met Christians who think that they can judge the eternal state of a person's soul, even when that person's lips heartily profess the opposite of their conclusion, and even when that person is a baptized member of the church. This is impossible, and wrong to attempt, because any such judgment necessarily rests on a knowledge that no man possesses about another—namely, what is in the heart (1 Cor. 4:5).

I would suggest that when someone has professed personal faith in Christ, been baptized in the name of the Father, Son, and Holy Spirit, and identified with the church, we are then under obligation from Scripture to make no negative judgments about the validity of his faith. That obligation remains even when a professing believer seems to exhibit a lack of fruit, or even if he commits repeated and heinous sin, because in those cases the other members of the body of Christ are called to encourage, admonish, and if necessary discipline him according to the process Jesus outlined in Matthew 18:15–17. Each of those means of sanctification are based on the presupposition that in most cases the Holy Spirit is present and operative in the sinner's life. Otherwise they could not be effective in helping that person to grow in grace and to put away the sin against which we all continue to struggle. And remember, it is only at the end of the process in Matthew 18 that Jesus says we should treat the sinner as an unbeliever![2]

But, someone might say, aren't we supposed to be "fruit inspectors"? Didn't Jesus Himself say, "You will know them by their fruits"? Well, the context of that verse (Matt. 7:20) is a discussion of false teachers, whom Jesus calls "wolves in sheep's clothing." He is giving us a way to discern whether we should follow certain teachers, and He is telling us not to follow those who bear bad fruit. There may be some conclusions we could reach about the spiritual state of such deceivers, but that is incidental to the point of the passage—the passage is clearly *not* about regular members of the body.

On the other hand, consider Paul's discussion of the incestuous and divisive man in 1 Corinthians 5. In verse 3 Paul says, "I . . . have already judged him," but the context makes clear that his judgment was merely that the man needed to be put out of the church (vv. 4–5). Paul's judgment was clearly *not* that the man was unsaved, even at that late stage of church discipline, because in verse 11 he calls the man a "so-called brother" (or literally "one who is called a brother").[3] Certainly after such a long period of boastful, unrepentant sin on his part, this man's salvation was questionable to some degree in Paul's mind, but Paul emphatically does not cross the judging line and say "put him out because he is not a Christian." If there ever was a prime candidate in the church to be thought of as a unbeliever, it was this man—yet Paul did not go that far.[4]

A similar scenario is found in 2 Thessalonians 3:6–15, where Paul commands that church to carry out the third step of church discipline, in which all the members of the church are to confront the sinner for his sin (cf. Matt. 18:17a). Because certain idle people had not responded to the clear admonishment of Paul and others (vv. 6, 10, 12), the members were to "keep away" or "withdraw themselves" from any sinning Christian "so that he will be put to shame" (vv. 6, 14). But notice how Paul closes his discussion in verse 15: "Yet do not regard him as an enemy, but admonish him as a brother." The Greek term for "regard" clearly denotes a mental attitude, and the term "enemy" (*echthros*) is often used as a synonym for "unbeliever" (cf. Rom. 5:10; Col. 1:21).[5] So this verse teaches us that we should never think of a member of the church as an unbeliever, even if he or she is sinning openly.

Finally, let us consider several more passages in Scripture that relate to this specific issue of forming an opinion about someone's salvation.

Matthew 13:27–30. In the parable of the wheat and tares, mentioned earlier, Jesus says this:

> The slaves of the landowner came and said to him, "Sir, did you not sow good seed in your field? How then does it have tares?" And he said to them, "An enemy has done this!" And the slaves said to him, "Do you want us, then, to go and gather them up?" But he said, "No; for while you are gathering up the tares, you may uproot the wheat with them. Allow both to grow together until the harvest; and in the time of the harvest I will say to the reapers, 'First gather up the tares and bind them in bundles to burn them up; but gather the wheat into my barn.' "

In this parable, the landowner (who represents God) tells the slaves (who represent us) not to try to separate the wheat from the tares before the appointed time of the harvest. So Jesus is basically telling us that we should not try to determine which members of the body are true believers, and which are false believers, because that will be made known only at the Judgment Day. He cannot be forbidding the practice of church discipline, because five chapters later, in Matthew 18:15–17, He tells us to do that. So His concern must be our tendency to try to separate the wheat from the tares by judging people's salvation. And notice the reason for His concern—if we judge one another in this way, we will uproot some wheat along with the tares. Such judgments will be seriously mistaken at times, causing unnecessary division between us and our fellow Christians. We will end up being separated from other true Christians, contrary to the Lord's command.

1 Corinthians 4:3–5. We discussed this passage at length in the early chapters of this book, but read it again now with the topic we are discussing in mind:

> To me it is a very small thing that I may be examined by you, or by any human court; in fact, I do not even examine myself. For I am conscious of nothing against myself, yet I am not by this acquitted; but the one who examines me is the Lord. Therefore do not go on passing judgment before the time, but wait until the Lord comes who will both bring to light the things hidden in the darkness and disclose the motives of men's hearts; and then each man's praise will come to him from God.

As we learned, the general occasion of this passage is the bickering of the Corinthians over whether Paul or Apollos was a better leader (3:3–4). But it is also apparent that the Corinthians had been sinfully judging Paul (4:3), because they were examining him on the basis of unbiblical standards (v. 6) and forming opinions about what was in his heart (v. 5). Could it be that they were thinking that he was a false apostle and therefore not a true Christian? The only hint that they might have been doing so lies in his use of the term "acquitted" (i.e., "justified") in verse 4—but that is not conclusive. Even if they were not judging his salvation, however, these verses leave us with a stern warning against that activity, because if the Corinthians were sinning by judging his apostleship or personal godliness, how much more wrong would we be to think that we can know whether someone is saved or not?! The command to "judge nothing" (lit., v. 5) means more than the issue of salvation, but it cannot mean any less than that.

Romans 14. This passage, which we also discussed earlier, is the most extensive passage in Scripture on the issue of judging, and it also pertains to the issue at hand (even though its scope is definitely broader). In this passage Paul is trying to stop the Romans from evaluating in their minds whether others in the church are "accepted by God," "standing before God," "living for the Lord," and "able to stand at the judgment seat of God." He also has to remind them that "*the kingdom of God* is not eating and drinking. . . ." This terminology seems to imply that at least some of them were forming judgments about the salvation of others. So these words of Paul apply to that issue: "Who are you to judge the servant of another?" (v. 4) and "Therefore let us not judge one another anymore" (v. 13).

James 4:11–12. This is the passage in Scripture that speaks most directly to the issue. After teaching his readers to examine *themselves* because "faith without works is dead" and cannot save (2:14–26), James warns them against shining that searchlight in the same way upon others:

> Do not speak against one another, brethren. He who speaks against a brother or judges his brother, speaks against the law and judges the law; but if you judge the law, you are not a doer of the law, but a judge of it. There is only one Lawgiver and Judge, the One who is able to save and to destroy; but who are you who judge your neighbor?

Only a prejudiced reader could conclude that this passage has no bearing on the issue of evaluating another's salvation. In the same breath that he upbraids his readers for judging one another, James makes a point of saying that there is only *"One who is able to save and to destroy."* Like Paul in 1 Corinthians 4, James does not leave us in the dark as to what kind of judging he is forbidding. He explains what he means in this way: we are not to set up standards above and beyond the revealed law (or based on an obscure interpretation of it),[6] and we are never to usurp the place of the one true Judge in deciding who among the brethren has been saved and who is heading for destruction.

We could discuss all those passages in much more depth, but hopefully you can see from this brief survey that we must be very careful not to wrongfully judge another person's faith in Christ. Perhaps more than any other judgment, that one builds a wall between members of the body that becomes almost impossible to tear down once it has been erected. So I encourage you again to submit all your thoughts and words to this familiar command of our Lord Jesus Christ: "Do not judge so that you will not be judged. For in the way you judge, you will be judged; and by your standard of measure, it will be measured to you" (Matt. 7:1–2). Think twice before you conclude that a fellow member of the body is not a true Christian. It is likely other critical people could find some reason to question *your* profession, if they knew you well enough!

Notes

Chapter One: The Case against Judging

1. Sometimes the terms "judge" and "judgment" are used (primarily in reference to God) to mean the *execution* of judgment as well as the judgment itself (e.g., 1 Cor. 11:30–32). Or to use court terminology, the meaning of the word "judgment" often includes the verdict *and* the punishment (e.g., John 3:17; Heb. 13:4). But many times the term is used to represent merely the mental process by which an individual decides that something is right or wrong (e.g., Luke 12:57; 1 Cor. 10:15; 11:13). In Luke 6:37, for instance, Jesus uses "judge" and "condemn" side by side—apparently He means by the first the inward opinion and by the second a more outward demonstration of that judgment.

2. Charles Spurgeon, *Treasury of David*, vol. 3 (Peabody, MA: Hendrickson, n.d.), 288.

3. Matthew Henry, *Matthew Henry's Commentary on the Whole Bible* (Peabody, MA: Hendrickson, 1991), 6:421.

Chapter Two: Judgment Day

1. Erwin Lutzer, *Who Are You to Judge? Learning to Distinguish between Truths, Half-Truths, and Lies* (Chicago: Moody, 2003). Another example is Jay E. Adams, *A Call for Discernment: Distinguishing Truth from Error in Today's Church* (Woodruff, SC: Timeless Texts, 1987).

2. The Greek verb *phōtisei* ("bring to light") is obviously revelation terminology, but so is *ta krypta* ("the things hidden"). Paul likes to use it when he speaks of divine revelation—for example, see Ephesians 3:9. He may have gotten the idea to use *ta krypta* from the famous verse Deuteronomy 29:29, where "the secret things," mentioned in contrast to the written Word, renders the Hebrew term *nistarot*, which in the Septuagint is translated by *kryptos*.

Notes

3. Even if "the things hidden in the darkness" is not a reference to matters outside of Scripture, my point about judging them still stands, because that is definitely Paul's concern in the next verse.

4. For an extended discussion about Christians and alcohol, see Kenneth Gentry's book *God Gave Wine: What the Bible Says about Alcohol* (Lincoln, CA: Oakdown Books, 2000).

5. Quoted in Paul Lee Tan, *Encyclopedia of 7700 Illustrations* (Chicago: R. R. Donnelley and Sons, 1979), 692.

6. This situation also illustrates how an atmosphere of judgmentalism and legalism can exist, even if it might be denied verbally. What I mean is that the pastor mentioned in the letter might say, if he was pressed, "I'm not saying it's a *sin* if you don't come to all the services." But yet this is the message he is essentially communicating. We must be careful to guard ourselves against any form of sinful judging, because we all can easily fall into it, even if that is not our intention.

Chapter Three: Cross-Examining Your Judgments

1. Examples of such prejudice between groups abound, but I recently read of one that is especially sad. Thomas Alan Harvey's book *Acquainted with Grief* (Grand Rapids: Brazos, 2002) tells the story of Wang Mingdao, the father of China's "house church" movement. To this day, the Chinese Christians in government-licensed churches are deeply suspicious and even resentful of those in the house churches, and vice versa. And it all started in the conflict over state licensing. Wang wrote about those who accepted licensing, "Many Christian leaders use the principle of obedience to man's rules and submission to man's authority to cover up their cowardice and failure" (p. 72). And his opponents fired back, "Wang Mingdao is a talented speaker, and some argue that he simply explains the Bible clearly and logically. In truth, his use of the Bible is purely politically motivated" (p. 78). Notice how both Wang and his opponents were assuming wrong motives on the part of those who disagreed with them. In many cases, they were probably wrong—some Chinese Christians were trying to honor God by obeying the government, others by separating from it. But they judged one another harshly, and the gap between them and between their followers only widened from there.

2. Bill Gothard has been teaching this for years in his Institute for Basic Youth Conflicts.

3. Dave Hunt criticized contemporary worship in his "Berean Call" newsletter by saying, "Sadly, today's 'worshippers' seem content to sing over and over, for example, 'I will sing of your love forever.' . . . To repeat, 'I will sing of your love forever,' is not singing of His love at all. You are only saying you are *going* to sing of His love. Stop *promising* to sing of His love and do it!" This is an amazing example of how blinding legalism can be, and how it "invalidates the Word of God" (Mark 7:8–13; see chapter 7), because the words Hunt is criticizing *come directly from the Bible*, where they are found *repeatedly*! God Himself inspired these words in Exodus 15:1; Judges 5:3; 2 Samuel 22:50; Psalms 7:17; 9:2; 13:6; 18:49; 27:6; 30:12; 57:7; 57:9; 59:17; 61:8; 71:22; 71:23; 75:9; 89:1; 92:4; 101:1; 104:33; 108:1; 108:3; 138:1; 144:9; 146:2; Romans 15:9; and Hebrews 2:12.

4. This command was given to Adam and Eve, and then to Noah's family, when they were the *only people* on the earth, so the application of this command may well be limited to its specific historical context. Also, the exact same command was given to the fish and the birds in Genesis 1:22. As any serious Bible student knows, great care must be taken when applying narrative passages, especially from the Old Testament, to our lives today. An important rule of interpretation is that "narrative is not normative." The primary purpose of narrative texts is to tell us what happened, not to tell us what to do.

5. The apostle Paul had an "open door" for ministry in 2 Corinthians 2:12–13, but he did not choose to go that way. Having an open door does not mean that you have to walk through it. Likewise, having an open womb does not mean that you have to have a baby! For an extended discussion of human freedom in decision making, and how it relates to God's sovereign will, see my book *Decisions, Decisions: How (and How Not) to Make Them* (Phillipsburg, NJ: P&R Publishing, 2003).

6. In case you think I am swinging at windmills with this illustration, I have some friends who are in a church that believes all non-Calvinists are lost because they are trusting in themselves and believing in a "false gospel." They say that people cannot be saved if they think that Jesus died for everyone. This is a failure to recognize the complexity of the human heart (we can believe the wrong things for the right reasons), and the nature of progressive sanctification (we all have errors in our theology, and will until we meet the Lord).

7. For more information on why the claims of the therapeutic establishment should be met with skepticism, see Peter Breggin, *Toxic Psychiatry* (New York: St. Martin's, 1994), *Talking Back to Prozac* (New

Notes

York: St. Martin's, 1994), and *Your Drug May Be Your Problem* (Cambridge, MA: Perseus, 2000).

8. Jay E. Adams, *From Forgiven to Forgiving* (Wheaton, IL: Victor, 1989), 23–24.

9. The texts of all Shakespeare's works are in the public domain. Speaking of Shakespeare, by the way, a case could be made that one of the main themes of his work is the problem of judging. Take one famous comedy, and a famous tragedy, as examples. *Much Ado about Nothing*, as the title indicates, is all about the bad consequences that occur when we believe a report about someone that is not true, without investigating the issue properly (Claudio judges and publicly accuses Hero of infidelity). And the same thing happens in *Othello*, as the title character ends up killing his wife, and taking his own life, all because of a false, hasty judgment that he made ("To be once in doubt, is once to be resolved"). *Hamlet*, on the other hand, contains a good example of getting all the facts before coming to a conclusion, as the prince of Denmark tests the claims of his father's ghost, first by using a play to "catch the conscience of the king," and then by eavesdropping on his uncle's confession. Hamlet knew that "foul deeds will rise, though all the earth o'erwhelm them to men's eyes," but he made sure he got all the facts before he took his revenge.

10. One very specific application of the grace of the cross lies in how we describe others when we are talking to them or about them. We tend to label people, especially if we are having difficulty with them, by generally describing their character with words like "selfish," "bigoted," "lazy," "undependable," or even "judgmental." But it would be so much more edifying to reserve positive terms for when we are describing their character in general, and use the negative terms only when we are confronting specific sins. This is how God refers to His people in the New Testament—He describes them as "saints," "beloved," "righteous," "children of God," etc., even though they often have specific problems that need to be addressed.

Chapter Four: Paul's Illustration and Definition of Legalism

1. For example, Chuck Swindoll's book *The Grace Awakening* (Dallas: Word, 1990) is a good book on this topic, but the author never actually provides a clear and complete definition of legalism, even though he spends over 300 pages talking about it.

2. From *The Sword of the Lord* magazine, April 28, 1989.

3. One commentator I read said something like, "five words are inserted whose meaning lies beyond recovery," and another called the phrase "unintelligible." But they were liberal scholars, who tend to label as a scribal addition anything they can't figure out. It seems that if it takes a little work to ascertain the meaning of a portion of the text, they assume it must have been added or corrupted. This approach is not an option for those who accept the integrity of Scripture, and the trustworthiness of the God who delivered and preserved it.

4. The KJV is "that ye might learn in us not to think of men above that which is written"; the NKJV is "that you may learn in us not to think beyond what is written"; the ESV is "that you may learn by us not to go beyond what is written"; and the NIV is "so that you may learn from us the meaning of the saying, 'Do not go beyond what is written.' "

5. C. K. Barrett, *A Commentary on the First Epistle to the Corinthians* (New York: Harper and Row, 1968), 106.

6. She also probably implied, if she did not directly state, that her other rules were universal moral standards (church attendance, dress styles, hair length, etc.). I don't deny that she loved her son, or even that the administration of that college loves their students, but I think that they all should have been more careful not to "go beyond what is written."

7. As far as we know, tobacco grew originally only in the Americas. Native Americans (Northern and Southern) used it from ancient times, but not any of the people to whom the Bible was written.

8. The body is mentioned in the same context, but what Paul says actually disproves the "smoking is a sin" idea. First Corinthians 6:18 says that "*every other sin* that a man commits is outside the body, but the immoral man sins against his own body." If Paul is concerned with the issue of harming our physical bodies, then clearly the only sin that he is thinking of in that regard is sexual sin. And when you think through his words logically and apply them to our topic, they would indicate either that smoking is not harmful to the body, or that smoking is not a sin.

9. For more information about the role of wisdom in non-sinful areas, and the "area of freedom" that exists outside of the clear commands of Scripture, see my book *Decisions, Decisions: How (and How Not) to Make Them* (Phillipsburg, NJ: P&R Publishing, 2003).

10. One of the authors starts to argue that gambling is a sin by chronicling its terrible effects on society. But remember that the same case of "guilt by association" can be made, and has been made, against things like alcohol use (look how many lives have been ruined!), contemporary music (look at the wickedness of the rock culture!), or even watch-

ing TV (Hollywood is so evil!). The fact that there is much abuse asso-
ciated with a particular practice does not mean that the practice is sinful in itself. Should we abandon all books because so much of the stuff
in the bookstore is trash?

11. I do not know about this personally, but a friend of mine told
me that games like poker require a lot of skill to win consistently, and
that some people earn money by using their skills to do so. This method
of gaining income is not unlike stock trading, and other similar forms
of "risky" business.

12. For instance, I have little or no desire to ever gamble again in
my life. (Yes, I am "Bill"—my middle name is William! A little secret
for those who actually take time to read the endnotes.) But my lack of
desire to gamble is not because I think gambling is a sin. It is because
God has worked in my heart to establish certain perspectives and pri-
orities, so that I would rather spend my time and money on other things.
Thus the key to the gambling issue is the heart—as it is with all the
issues of life (Prov. 4:23).

Chapter Five: Two Dangers of Legalism

1. Chuck Swindoll, *The Grace Awakening* (Dallas: Word, 1990), 77.

2. The singular "you" in the next verse also supports the universal
intent of this verse. Paul is not talking about groups of people forming
into factions, but any individual who makes unbiblical judgments.

3. One of the arguments I have heard for weekly communion is that
Paul begins his discussion of the Lord's Supper in 1 Corinthians 11:20
by saying, "When you meet together," implying that the Corinthians
always had communion when they met together (especially in light of
v. 18). But even if the Corinthians had communion every Sunday, that
does not mean that we have to do so, in the absence of such a command from the Lord. And the instruction that Paul gives in this passage is not concerned with the frequency of communion at all, but with
how it is observed. Notice in 1 Corinthians 11:33 that he says, "When
you come together *to eat. . . .*" He is concerned with what we do when
we come to the table, not how often we do it.

4. Jeffrey J. Meyers, *The Lord's Service* (Moscow, ID: Canon Press,
2003), 213–14. I appreciate much of what Meyers says in this book,
even about the nature and importance of the Lord's Supper. But he
fails to prove his assertion that God has commanded us to observe it
every Sunday. The fact that the Lord's Supper is a covenant memorial,

for instance, does not mean that it has to be practiced weekly. Everything Meyers says about the supper in this regard was also true of Passover, yet it was observed only once a year.

5. I will discuss the education issue in chapter 10, but the paedocommunion issue is another one addressed by Jeffrey Meyers in his book *The Lord's Service.* Meyers clearly implies that it is morally wrong for us to withhold communion from our very young children because they cannot examine themselves or "discern the body" (1 Cor. 11:28–29). He even goes so far as to say that we who do so are the ones who should be barred from the table (p. 395)! He compares the practice of most Christians in history to people who "despised the Church of God" (1 Cor. 11:22) and the disciples with whom Christ was "indignant" (Mark 10:14). The irony of this is that Meyers could have made a case for the *allowance* of paedocommunion, based on the principle I am talking about in this book. But as it is, he becomes legalistic himself by saying that little children *must* be given communion, and he even twists the Scripture to make his point. For instance, on page 394 he says that 1 Corinthians 11:29 ("discern the body") condemns traditional Presbyterians because they do not give the bread and wine to little children. But as Meyers asserts repeatedly in his exegesis, the passage was not intended to address the issue of children at all!

Chapter Six: Pride Questioned and Convicted

1. Quoted in *Spurgeon at His Best*, compiled by Tom Carter (Grand Rapids: Baker Book House, 1988), 165.

2. Ibid.

3. Special Rider Music, copyright 1965, renewed 1993.

4. R. C. Lenski, *The Interpretation of St. Paul's First and Second Epistles to the Corinthians* (Minneapolis: Augsburg, 1961), 177.

5. Gordon Fee, *1 Corinthians*, in the New International Commentary on the New Testament (Grand Rapids: Eerdmans, 1987), 171.

6. Charles Spurgeon, *The Metropolitan Tabernacle Pulpit*, vol. 22, page 6 (taken from *The C. H. Spurgeon Collection* CD, published by Ages Software).

7. Ibid., pages 10–11.

8. John Fischer, *12 Steps for a Recovering Pharisee (Like Me)* (Grand Rapids: Bethany House, 2000), 145–46.

Chapter Seven: Jesus and Legalism

1. Robert Coleman, *The Pharisees' Guide to Total Holiness* (Minneapolis: Bethany House, 1977), 8–10.

2. Ibid., 13–14.

3. Chuck Swindoll, *The Grace Awakening* (Dallas: Word, 1990), 96–97.

4. Coleman, *Pharisees' Guide*, 8.

5. Swindoll, *Grace Awakening*, 49.

6. Ibid.

7. John MacArthur, *Matthew 8–15* in the MacArthur New Testament Commentary Series (Chicago: Moody, 1987), 282.

8. For a further discussion of this idea, and all the biblical principles related to decision making, see the author's book *Decisions, Decisions: How (and How Not) to Make Them* (Phillipsburg, NJ: P&R Publishing, 2003).

9. Carl F. H. Henry, *Christian Personal Ethics* (Grand Rapids: Eerdmans, 1957), 421.

10. In Leviticus 23:27 and other verses God commands the Israelites to "humble themselves" or "afflict themselves" on the Day of Atonement. Most commentators believe this is a reference to fasting.

11. This is a quote from the 1536 edition of Calvin's *Institutes*, Section 23.

12. Richard Gaffin, *Calvin and the Sabbath* (Fearn, Ross-shire, Great Britain: Mentor Books, 1998), 49–50. The quote is from the 1536 edition of Calvin's *Institutes*, Section 23. In his commentary on Isaiah 58:13–14, Calvin says that the prophet "shows clearly that the true observation of the Sabbath consists in self-denial and thorough conversion. . . . For he contemplated something higher than an outward ceremony, that is indolence and repose, in which the Jews thought that the greatest holiness consisted. On the contrary, he commanded the Jews to renounce the desires of the flesh, to give up their sinful inclinations, and to yield obedience to him; as no man can meditate on the heavenly life, unless he be dead to the world and to himself. Now, although the ceremony has been abolished, nevertheless the truth remains; because Christ died and rose again, so that we have a continual Sabbath; that is we are released from our works, that the Spirit of God may work mightily in us" (quoted in Gaffin, 90–91).

Chapter Eight: What to Do When Someone Is Different from You

1. Some might think that the Word of God speaks to this issue in Acts 15:20, where James articulates the decisions of the Jerusalem council, and its advice to the Gentile converts. There he says the church should tell the Gentiles to "abstain from things contaminated by idols," as the NASB translates it. That might be taken to be an authoritative statement about eating meat offered to idols. But in light of the later statements of Paul, and the Greek grammar in the verse, a better translation would be "abstain from the pollutions of idols," as the NASB marginal note reads. James is simply saying they should not participate in idol worship, an issue that was clearly biblical, like all the other issues he mentions in his declaration (v. 20).

2. This verse is another reason why I believe the Sabbath issue falls squarely into the topic of this book, because not only did Jesus make a big deal of it, but Paul also brings it into his discussion here, and in Colossians 2. Why should we be surprised if Christians throughout history, and even in our day, are legalistic in some way regarding the Lord's Day?

3. Some commentators suggest that in this passage Paul is referring to an unbeliever when he talks about someone raising questions of conscience. In that case the intent of the passage would be similar to that of 1 Corinthians 9:19–23, where Paul discusses the idea of limiting our freedom for the sake of evangelism. But even if the passage I'm discussing is taken that way, it still illustrates the fact that our application of the principle of edification must be *situational* rather than universal.

4. Garry Friesen, *Decision Making and the Will of God* (Portland, OR: Multnomah, 1980), 416.

5. If we take the verse this way, there is a scriptural basis for keeping some things that we do just among close friends, or people that we know will not be offended or tempted by them. But even if the Bible does not tell us to do that explicitly, I would suggest it is still a wise policy. We are not hypocrites merely because we do not tell everyone about everything we do—but only if we present ourselves as something we are not.

6. If we take the "he" who is approving to refer to the person who is condemning himself, then Paul would seem to be contradicting himself. But even if this is a play on words, and Paul is referring to the person rather than God, the point is still basically the same.

7. For more verses about the importance of having a clean conscience, see Acts 23:1 and 24:16; 1 Timothy 1:9; and Hebrews 13:18.

8. The passage most often used to support this idea is Deuteronomy 22:5, which is talking about the perverted practice of transvestitism. It certainly is not meant to address pants, because both men and women wore skirt-like robes and tunics at the time (nobody wore pants!). And when it comes to the New Testament teaching on modesty, the fact is that in many situations pants are more modest than dresses are. So although it is fine for a particular woman to decide that she will not wear pants, she should never present that as a universal moral standard or judge others who do not share her conviction.

Chapter Nine: Case Study 1: Entertainment and the Popular Arts

1. One of my seminary professors referred to the heart as the "mission control center" of our being. It represents the immaterial part of man, with special emphasis on the fact that it is the source of our "thoughts and intentions" (Gen. 6:5; cf. Prov. 4:23 and 23:7).

2. T. M. Moore, "Why Art Matters," article on the BreakPoint Web site, posted February 27, 2004.

3. Most of what I say in this chapter could also be applied to a Christian's involvement in sports, another issue that is sometimes the occasion for judging and legalism (Kuiper is an example; see n. 4). If you would like to consider that issue further, I recommend an article by Dr. Lee Smith entitled "Sports—A Biblical Perspective," which is posted on his church's Web site at www.randolphefree.org.

4. Dale Kuiper's "The Christian and Entertainment" is posted on the web at www.prca.org in the articles section. Kuiper is a minister in the Protestant Reformed Church.

5. Charles Spurgeon, *The Treasury of David*, vol. 2 (Peabody, MA: Hendrickson, n.d.), 240.

6. To say that single people should never think about love and sex would be to say that they should never read the Song of Solomon, one of the books in the Bible.

7. Again, this does not mean that it is necessarily wrong to watch *Batman*, any more than it is wrong to watch *Bibleman*. We just need to make sure that our hearts do not rejoice in the evil depicted.

8. I remember renting the movie *Pulp Fiction*, because a Christian friend told me it was his favorite film ever. I kept waiting for some kind of redemptive value to grace the screen, but nothing even came close. So I vowed that I would never waste two hours of my life watching that movie again, even though it was interesting in a sick sort of way, and

funny at times. So many movies are like that—they are slick and well-made by cinematic standards, but have no profit in them whatsoever. As someone has pointed out, movie critics and fans are always commenting on whether a movie is made well, but never stop to ask *why* it was made in the first place! What's the *point* of a movie like that, except to find amusement in evil and make money for the people who produce it? Christians should learn to ask that kind of question more often.

9. Someone once defined discipleship as "a friendship for spiritual purposes." I think that is a helpful definition, because it reminds us that we don't have to be studying the Bible at every moment to be making disciples.

10. For further consideration of this principle in Matthew 5:29–30, see Jay E. Adams, *A Theology of Christian Counseling* (Grand Rapids: Zondervan, 1979), chap. 16.

11. This dynamic is one of the reasons that legalism regarding entertainment is so prevalent, especially among young or immature believers. Many of them probably do need to distance themselves from the entertainment of the world, or build some fences in their own life, until they can grow stronger spiritually. But the problem arises when they transfer their fences to everyone else, and accept or promote the teaching that everyone else must live by their standards. Likewise, the problem with my college was not the strict rules for the students (I can see a certain wisdom in that), but the teaching and implication that the rules were divine standards equal to the commands of Scripture.

Chapter Ten: Case Study 2: Public Education

1. From the Minutes of the 3rd Presbytery Meeting of the C.R.E., posted on their Web site at www.crepres.org.

2. These books are Douglas Wilson, *Recovering the Lost Tools of Learning* (Wheaton, IL: Crossway, 1991), *Excused Absence: Should Christian Kids Leave Public Schools?* (Mission Viejo, CA: Crux Press, 2001), and *The Case for Classical Christian Education* (Wheaton, IL: Crossway, 2003). He also makes his case against public schools in chapter 7 of *Standing on the Promises* (Moscow, ID: Canon Press, 1997).

3. Wilson, *Standing on the Promises*, 92–93.

4. Wilson, *Excused Absence*, 39.

5. As I discussed earlier in chapter 8, note 1, I believe that a thorough examination of the council's directions to the churches reveals that they refused to go beyond what is written. It seems that they were

confronted with a list of dos and don'ts by the Judaizers, and they chose to enforce only the dos and don'ts that were clearly scriptural requirements. Interestingly enough, they omitted typological observances like circumcision and the Sabbath, but retained the timeless biblical prohibitions against idolatry, uncooked meat, and sexual immorality.

6. Wilson, *Excused Absence*, 60.

7. Ibid.

8. I know just enough formal logic to be dangerous, because I'm teaching a class in it this year for the first time. And guess what textbook I am using: *Introductory Logic*, by Douglas Wilson! *Petitio principii* is discussed on page 112.

9. Here are a few interesting examples from Wilson's writings: First, in *Recovering the Lost Tools of Learning* he says, "Although there is no 'sin' called 'sending kids to public school,' the moral responsibilities of parents with regard to education are considerable. . . . These considerations, taken together, do indicate that a good Christian education is a moral necessity" (p. 55). Wilson is speaking out of both sides of his mouth here—he says it is not a sin (in quotation marks), but then he says it is a matter of "moral necessity." Is failing in a moral necessity not a sin?

Likewise, in *Standing on the Promises* he writes, "Nowhere does the Bible label as sin the practice called 'sending a child to government school.' Consequently, we must imitate the Scriptures in this. At the same time, the Bible is very clear on the central parental responsibility in education, and this *principle*, when applied to our contemporary situation, provides us with clear direction" (p. 91). What Wilson is basically saying is that the Bible doesn't say *in so many words* that sending children to public school is a sin, but the Bible is clear that it is a sin.

And finally, in an e-mail response to the manuscript of this book, Wilson said, "I completely agree there is no sin called 'receiving instruction of some kind from an unbeliever.' I just believe it is a sin when the recipient is unprotected and ill-equipped." I find this to be a good way of addressing the issue—better than the approach he uses in some of his writings. But even here it is important to recognize that it is difficult to measure when a particular student is "unprotected and ill-equipped," and so we must be careful not to make universal applications of this principle. Again, my suggestion is to teach the principle and leave the application to individual parents.

10. The full text of this resolution can be found at www.getthekidsout .org.

11. This resolution is also posted at the Web site above.

Conclusion: Legalism and the Gospel

1. The legalistic churches and schools in my background all seemed to have a view of the gospel that was largely man-centered, regarding decisions for Christ as basically equivalent to saving faith, and implying that repentance involves a surrender to the external rules of the system. For example, one evangelist's message to my high school was basically, "If you want to be a Christian, pray this sinner's prayer with me and dump your rock and roll records in the trash can." As often as he might have said we are saved by faith alone, the impression he gave was clearly the opposite. And on another point of the spectrum, in the Reformed world, it is interesting to note that Douglas Wilson and others adhering to the "Federal Vision," who I believe are legalistic about several Christian life issues, have been accused of mixing faith with works in a way similar to the "New Perspective on Paul." I have seen no evidence that they are heretical in their views on salvation, but even if they are being misunderstood, this may be another example of a relationship between legalism and the way the gospel is articulated.

2. Harry L. Reeder III with David Swavely, *From Embers to a Flame: How God Can Revitalize Your Church* (Phillipsburg, NJ: P&R Publishing, 2004), 68–69.

Appendix: The Ultimate Human Judgment

1. For a more thorough discussion of how church membership is connected with this issue, see chapters 1 and 2 in Wayne Mack and Dave Swavely, *Life in the Father's House: A Member's Guide to the Local Church* (Phillipsburg, NJ: P&R Publishing, 1996).

2. The Greek text of Matthew 18:17 is somewhat ambiguous as to whether Jesus meant to *consider* an excommunicated person as an unbeliever, or whether He meant to *treat* the individual that way (the literal translation is "let him be to you . . . "). The latter is a much more acceptable interpretation, because in the rest of the passage Jesus is not telling us how to think about someone, but how to act toward him. It is hard to imagine Jesus condoning the prejudicial, hateful *attitude* that the Jews held toward the Gentiles and publicans, but it is conceivable that He would command the *action* of removal from membership and refusal of fellowship.

3. Also consider Paul's intention in delivering the man to Satan—so that his flesh might be destroyed and his spirit saved (v. 5). This clearly

implies that the man may be a true believer who needs the chastening of his heavenly Father to bring him back to holiness (Heb. 12:5–11).

4. It is always right to challenge a congregation to examine themselves (2 Cor. 13:5), and in some cases it is prudent to question the profession of an individual brother whom we know well. But to apply what we learned earlier in the book under the definition of "judging," there is a significant difference between wondering about whether people are truly saved and deciding that they are not. According to Paul's example and teaching, the first is biblically acceptable (in some cases), but the second is never acceptable.

5. In fact, *echthros* was used widely in Hellenistic Jewish literature to refer to Gentiles, and of course used by Jesus and Paul in the New Testament to mean "unbelievers." The *Theological Dictionary of the New Testament*, ed. Gerhard Kittel and Gerhard Friedrich, trans. Geoffrey W. Bromiley, abridged ed. (Grand Rapids: Eerdmans, 1985), says, "Basic to the usage is that Gentiles do not alternate between hostility and friendship but are in constant opposition to both Israel and God (Exodus 23:22)" (p. 285).

6. This has to be James's meaning when he refers to the law, because he cannot be rebuking his readers for examining someone's actions in light of that code. He has written already in 1:25 that it is the duty of every man to abide in that "perfect law."

Index of Scripture

Dave Swavely (M.Div.) is a teaching elder in the Presbyterian Church in America. He was the founding pastor of Faith Church in Sonoma, California, and he is currently planting a church in the Malvern area near Philadelphia.

He has also written *Decisions, Decisions: How (and How Not) to Make Them*. He coauthored, with Wayne A. Mack, *Life in the Father's House: A Member's Guide to the Local Church* and, with Harry L. Reeder, *From Embers to a Flame: How God Can Revitalize Your Church*.